M000190061

"This book will _____ _____
you see your business."

MARSHALL GOLDSMITH - THINKERS 50 #1 EXECUTIVE COACH

PLAY

HOW TO WIN IN TODAY'S

THE

CHANGING ENVIRONMENT

GAME

ADAM STRONG

+ 17 GAME-CHANGING LEADERS

Play the Game

First published in 2021 by

Panoma Press Ltd
48 St Vincent Drive, St Albans, Herts, AL1 5SJ, UK
info@panomapress.com
www.panomapress.com

Book layout by Neil Coe.

978-1-784529-53-6

The rights of Adam Strong, Akhtar Khan, Allan Kleynhans, Branka van der Linden, Chris Cooper, Darrell Wayne Irwin, David Burgess, Don Sandel, Haroon Danis, Heather Margaret Barrie, Hilary Humphrey, Karel Vermeulen, Mehdi Ettehadulhagh, Michael Robison, Sarah Franklin, Stefan Tonnon, Stephen Carter and Vicky Poole to be identified as the authors of this work have been asserted in accordance with sections 77 and 78 of the Copyright, Designs and Patents Act 1988.

A CIP catalogue record for this book is available from the British Library.

All rights reserved. No part of this book may be reproduced in any material form (including photocopying or storing in any medium by electronic means and whether or not transiently or incidentally to some other use of this publication) without the written permission of the copyright holder except in accordance with the provisions of the Copyright, Designs and Patents Act 1988. Applications for the copyright holder's written permission to reproduce any part of this publication should be addressed to the publishers.

This book is available online and in bookstores.

Copyright 2021 Adam Strong, Akhtar Khan, Allan Kleynhans, Branka van der Linden, Chris Cooper, Darrell Wayne Irwin, David Burgess, Don Sandel, Haroon Danis, Heather Margaret Barrie, Hilary Humphrey, Karel Vermeulen, Mehdi Ettehadulhagh, Michael Robison, Sarah Franklin, Stefan Tonnon, Stephen Carter and Vicky Poole.

TESTIMONIALS

"*Play the Game* will radically change the way you see your business! Adam's powerful stories and insights illustrate the true foundation of entrepreneurship. Read this book and start growing your business today!"

Marshall Goldsmith - Thinkers 50 #1 Executive Coach and only two-time #1 Leadership Thinker in the world

"If only I had read this book before I sold my last company – I would have had the skills to keep it! This is a candy store of knowledge, packed with so many ways to achieve success. This is key, as we will all have a unique formula to unlock the doors to our own journey of wealth and happiness. But, as Adam Strong says, 'Asking for help is a sign of strength, not a weakness.' It took me 40 years to ask for help! I really enjoyed the read and am applying many of the techniques right now from this hugely informative and inspirational book to make my new chocolate television series finally happen."

Angus Kennedy, Author, Speaker and Celebrity Chocolate Expert

"Fantastic read. Straight-forward success concepts to adapt to change and empowering readers to align to their 'why' and what works best for them to apply in their lives."

Chris Salem, CEO, Business Advisor and award-winning Author

"As a business owner myself I know too well what it feels like when you get stuck. Business is like a game: we often make it difficult for ourselves and therefore need a new perspective. The stories in this book highlight what entrepreneurship stands for. If you want to take your business to the next level, then this book is a must-read."

Tracey Smolinski, Founder of Introbiz, Co-Founder of IWOW and Author of *Master Networking*

"I've read hundreds of business books over the years and one thing is for sure: this book covers all of the points you will need to run a successful business and maintain a positive mindset! There are some immutable laws of success in life and business; I'm not talking about laws that the government set, these are laws that are there whether you believe them or even know about them. Just like gravity, if you fall from the top of a building in the UK or in New York City you will fall to the ground at the same rate of acceleration regardless of your beliefs. This book covers those laws in one way or another and your job is to hunt them down and then action them. Unless of course you're not serious about your business?"

Ash Lawrence, Sports Psychologist, Business Owner and Founder of the Millionaire Mindset and ABC Network

FOREWORD

I am one luckiest guys I know because I am the son of John Dalton Elton.

My dad was one of those people that you just loved being around. When you were with 'Dalt' you knew it was going to be fun. You were going to laugh, hear some incredible stories and probably break out into song at some point. It was like being in a Broadway play spending time with my dad. He was my best friend, my cheerleader, my inspiration and the best role model a kid could ever hope for. I think about him and miss him every day. Even now he inspires me to be a better husband, father and friend. His example helped me to grow. His story changed my life.

The best part of being with my dad is that it wasn't all about him. In fact, most of the time, it would be all about you. See he knew that everyone has a story – and that is the most important story in the world – and he wanted to hear it. Stories mattered to my dad, and they should matter to all of us. They connect us, they teach us and they inspire us. Once you know someone's story, everything changes. Emotional bonds and understanding happen, and we all come together when we know where we have come from, how we got here and most importantly where we want to go!

That's why this book by my friend Adam Strong is so important. It is a book of stories of some of the most amazing people you will ever read about. They aren't just people that Adam has found in Google searches; these are people he knows well, has coached and has helped grow into the kind of people we can all aspire to be. Their stories will help you write your story.

You won't relate to every journey and every person you read about, but what you will find is that in each chapter there is a lesson on living life with purpose and passion. That when you are true to yourself and who you are at your core you can achieve great things in business and more importantly in life.

This isn't a book you have to read in sequence. You can pick it up and read any section and find a lesson, a plan, a tip, a tactic that could help you get to where you want to be like they did. Each person's journey will help you along yours.

My favorite part of the book is when Adam wraps it all up in a bow and gives you a step-by-step masterclass in how to succeed in your business. He will ask you three important questions:

1. What's important to you?

2. What are your strengths and weaknesses?

3. What are you passionate about?

And then he takes you on a trip that will help you grow and succeed and make your story one of inspiration and happiness.

My hope is that this book will in some small way be your John Dalton Elton. That it will help you grow to be a better leader, a better partner, a better person.

So read, ponder and start your writing story now!

Chester Elton

The Apostle of Appreciation and Best-Selling Author of *The Carrot Principle, Leading with Gratitude and Anxiety At Work*

CONTENTS

INTRODUCTION

There are boutique branding agencies out there that have clients who pay high-end prices. There are consultants out there who have partnered with influencers and industry thought leaders. There are property investors out there who get the most lucrative deals before they come out. There are skin care clinics out there that expand in a down market. There are lawyers out there who have a three-to-six-month waiting list to work with them. There are products out there that have customers who have pre-paid in advance even though the product doesn't exist yet.

How you ever wondered how some businesses and entrepreneurs have thrived during a downturn in the economy whereas most struggle to survive? Was it talent, faith or down to pure luck?

This book is designed to help established business owners and entrepreneurs like you break the cycle that stops your business from growing. It will help you to identify and overcome self-sabotaging habits, teach you how to create a thriving culture from the ground up and empower you to let go!

Throughout my years of being in business I have noticed that from experience businesses go through cycles of growth, and after a period of growth they begin to plateau and get sucked into a cycle that can keep them there for months if not years.

Back in 2020, I met a lady called Ellie (not her real name) who ran her own accountancy practice. She built a good reputation from her previous employment, was competent at what she did and was paid well. The problem with Ellie was that when she got near to her maximum capacity, she simply didn't have a clue how to take the business to the next level. She became overwhelmed with the volume of business that was coming in and trying to be everything to everyone.

We established that she needed to create a vision for herself and her business, put in place some simple systems and processes, recruit a team of three (two more accountants for sales and one admin person) and establish a thriving culture based on core values. Within a couple of months she recruited two accountants and an admin person allowing her to grow her practice to over £500,000, free herself from some of the day-to-day operational running of the business, and allow her to have the freedom and flexibility to do the things she enjoyed other than running a business.

What would have happened to Ellie's accountancy practice if she decided not to get the necessary help that she needed?

Have you ever been stuck in your business? How did it make you feel?

This book is designed to help you:

1. Monetise your purpose and passion with confidence

2. Create clarity without confusion

3. Shift your mindset and get you to look at your business from the top down

4. Become an empowered leader without feeling insecure

5. Accelerate your results by becoming accountable

6. Break the cycle that stunts your business growth

7. Speed up your decision-making by eliminating any false limiting beliefs you may have

This book showcases some of the amazing game-changers that have realised their true potential and have turned into more than just individuals as part of the process. There are some core values that I live by every day: to be authentic, show compassion towards others and to offer value. This empowers business owners and entrepreneurs to become the best versions of themselves.

Established entrepreneurs and business owners are very good at what they do. However, when their business gets close to capacity, they simply just stay busy, getting stuck working in the business and not on it. You work harder, not smarter. The business relies on you. You get stuck in a cycle and eventually fall out of love with what you do. This book will help you to create the breakthroughs needed to create impact and to scale your business with the ideas and solutions that you can offer the world.

My vision is to create 100,000 entrepreneurial-based businesses that want to become purpose-led, scalable and fun. One of the ways in which I choose to show up is by continuing to serve without expectation: the more I give the more the universe rewards me. By applying the principals in this book, everyone benefits, from your employees who want to become part of a thriving culture, to attracting top talent and retaining 'A' players in your company.

Becoming a game-changer helps you to become more innovative and adaptable, not insecure and frustrated. It helps you to focus on delivering the wow factor to your existing clients rather than chasing new ones and enables you to live your purpose rather than fall out of passion for it.

I know the struggles of being an entrepreneur and I share compassion and empathy because being a business owner or an entrepreneur isn't easy. You have to be prepared to ride the entrepreneurial rollercoaster, there will be highs and lows. This is what makes you become stronger and resilient.

The world moves so fast and we are all under pressure to deliver results. One thing I love about entrepreneurship is our ability to be adaptable and nimble and to get back up after being knocked down time and time again. By the end of this book, you will have the tools and resources to help you feel empowered creating awareness of your strengths and weaknesses as a leader enabling you to build a business that is fuelled with passion, love and alignment.

Each chapter is written by rising stars that have all come from different walks of life and have something to offer the world. This book isn't just full of inspirational stories, it begins by addressing your mindset and helping you to approach your business with a different perspective. You might want to read this book multiple times, formulate new ideas and implement the tactics and strategies to create impact and scale fast.

After publishing two previous books, I came to the realisation that we all desire and deserve happiness, success and fun which is why I believe in the power of collaboration. A tribe of people all working towards a common goal.

Why do it alone when you can do it together?

Let's do this together.

PLAY THE GAME

INSPIRATION ON DEMAND

DR MEHDI ETTEHADULHAGH

Picture this: 1992, Cameroon. A kid is born into a middle class household in one of the most corrupt third world countries on earth. Plagued with child soldiers, a pseudo-dictatorship government, broken health systems and devoid of educational infrastructure. One could say, in the lottery of life, I picked the short straw straight from day one. These were the cards life dealt me.

Fast forward to the present day, age 28. A freelance actor, former national athlete, serial entrepreneur in Norway, working simultaneously as the lead physician at a geriatrics centre with 160 patients, innovator and co-owner of 'VOTWEAR', the world's first muscle hypertrophy-accelerating SmartWear company, owner of one of the leading podcast studios in Scandinavia, 'Nordic Podcast Studios', and founder of a non-profit pre-school in Romania that's over five years old at the time of writing this. The reason I am starting the chapter in this manner is to make something crystal clear: I would never have made it this far without one particular lesson, which taught me the most valuable resource a human can possess, despite the economic, social and geographical conditions in which life begins.

So, what was this resource, the fuel that got me out of a third world country and mindset, cultivating me to grow beyond my outwardly-perceived potential at the time, taking me this far, despite my lack of exceptionalism in skills, knowledge, intelligence, generational wealth, nepotism-based network, or even business savvy? Frankly, I'm quite average. The resource behind my growth is simple and most importantly can be taught and utilised by anyone in any class, race, nationality, gender or country of residence. This resource is the foundation for all innovation and growth, it's the fuel that propels mankind forward. Learning this will be the foundation for changing your mind, body and soul within the game you inhabit daily, may it be professional or domestic. In short, this resource is the ability to summon systematically, predictably and consistently inspiration through meditation and then action. In other words, the secret method of practising 'inspiration on demand'.

Remember Who You Are

To truly harness the full potential of any tool, the first step is the recognition of the tool. If you look at a knife and see a weapon, that's the extent of its use, but if you see a tool that with education and guidance would magnify service in the culinary world, thus feeding countless people, its potential suddenly explodes, and you stop seeing a weapon, but instead an ally to endless growth and service. Which brings us to the question: as a tool, who are you, and what education and guidance reveals your true potential?

I believe the truth lies in history. Looking back, we clearly see that mankind is always progressing. Especially in knowledge and mental capacity. We see that these attributes come to humans a lot easier than to any other species on the planet, as well as the different channels in which these attributes, knowledge and skills come to us, in fields of language, science, art and even philosophy. Biologically, we resemble chimps, we are more than just the physical outer flesh, for when it comes to the intellect and the tether to inspiration we possess, we quickly see we are on a completely different level, bound by different rules, playing a different game in creation.

Categorising our entire civilisation as nothing more than that of advanced apes is seeing a knife as a weapon and not its full potential, overlooking the essence and the origin of our unique power, which is the human spirit. For man is in reality a being of the spirit; only when man thinks and operates in the spirit will his true potential be made manifest and this is the first step towards understanding why inspiration can be tapped; it's literally in the word 'inspiration'. It's 'in' the 'spirit' and it is through this faculty that all innovation, inventions and breakthroughs of mankind derive from.

Inspiration and Being of the Spirit

We all are familiar with the story of how Thomas Edison invented the incandescent light bulb. Previously, he succeeded only in passing electricity through a thin platinum filament in a glass vacuum bulb, barely lasting a few hours. Attempting over 6,000 different filaments and materials, he was caught saying this after finding success: "The electric light bulb has caused me the greatest amount of study and has required the most elaborate experiments; I was never myself discouraged or inclined to be hopeless of success. Genius is one percent inspiration, and ninety-nine percent perspiration." But oh, how he was wrong! The filament that burned the longest was created when Edison was not actively working or due to perspiration, but rather, in a meditative state, being guided and inspired. For Edison was sitting in his laboratory, with his hand on his desk, rocking mindlessly in his chair, his workstation was full of most compounds and materials, and absent-mindedly, he compressed a piece of carbon between his fingers and the carbonised-based filament was accidentally created and the 'New Type Edison Lamp Patent' was filed on January 27th 1880.

In what mental state was Edison when he got inspired to accidentally compress carbon? Can it be studied or replicated? We know through today's EEG research that there are five major brainwave states: Delta, Theta, Alpha, Beta and Gamma. These different states all serve a function, all can be induced on demand through either internal or external stimuli. The brainwave Theta (4-8Hz) strongly dominates our formative years, the years which children learn the majority of their social and language skills. But during the teenage years and deep into our adult lives, Theta waves become tightly correlated to creativity, insight, and inspiration. It's also the state that visits us as adults again during REM sleep, reduced consciousness and deep meditation. Much like Edison when he was mindlessly rocking in his chair, the solution of compressed carbon was given to him, a solution that didn't come to him in his hours of perspiration, but in the minutes of inspiration, despite him attributing perspiration to 99% of his genius.

But this doesn't explain the source of inspiration, only the state in which we need to be to get inspired. Like summoning the strike of lightning with a key and a kite, we understand the state required to attract lightning, but what is the source of the lightning? It's neither the key nor the kite, so the knowledge in which one is offered via inspiration isn't from ourselves, but from another source.

Power of Post Meditative Action

Being raised a Baha'i, a religion that believes in the oneness of all religions and the foundation of civilisation being built on science and religion going hand-in-hand, the knowledge of man being primarily a spiritual being, but in an ape-like body, was a reality that was easy to connect to at a young age: the Theta stage of my upbringing. I thus learned to use this as my substrate to go forth and harness inspiration through specific steps I will later share in this chapter. I quickly discovered that humans couldn't do two things at once, man can't speak and get inspired. Output can't be ongoing as input is received. So, while you meditate, while you enter a Theta state of no output, you become Ben Franklin's key and kite to inspiration. For in that state of mind, the source of inspirational lightning is indeed your own spirit. In that state of mind, you put certain questions to your spirit, your higher self, and it answers. This is a unique ability only witnessed in man and the driving force of our entire civilisation, for without this faculty, there is nothing separating us from our physical cousins, the chimpanzee.

This meditative state is like a mirror to which we are able to turn whatever we want, meaning if you are meditating upon material subjects, you will be informed of these. If you are meditating upon objects of the spirit and elevated thoughts that feed your higher self, and not one's ego, you will be informed of this as well. So, keep your Theta mind elevated to higher loftier subjects, and this is how your kite will get the altitude it needs to summon lightning time and time again.

Now that you understand who you are, your full potential, Theta states and why we maximise it through meditation, to make it less abstract, I will share the 'how' in the form of an exercise. Turning any desire into action is the greatest form of prayer there is, for what is prayer if not a selfless want or need that is manifested through action?

Exercise: Five Steps of Inspiration on Demand

Next are the five steps of inspiration on demand, the substrate inspired from the Baha'i writings and utilised to extract potential beyond my own:

Step 1: Pray and meditate about it. Then remain in the silence of contemplation weighing the different decisions for a few minutes.

Step 2: Through contemplation, arrive at a decision and hold it. No matter how far-fetched of an accomplishment or step, if it seems to be the answer to solving the problem, accept it as fact and take the next step.

Step 3: Having determination to carry this decision through. Most fail here. Decisions budding into determination prevent this phase from turning into merely a vague wish or longing. Take the next step only when determination is born.

Step 4: Have both faith and confidence that inspiration will flow through you, or the path will appear, the right door will open, the right thought, message, principle, or book will be given to you. That confidence will summon the right thing to come to your need. Now stand up, and take the final step through action.

Step 5: Action. Acting as though it had all already been answered and materialised.

Acting with grit and relentless energy. As you act, you, yourself, will become the magnet which will attract more inspiration and power to you, until you become the intended unobstructed channel for divine inspirational power to flow through you.

Follow and practise these steps of 'inspiration on demand'. They served me, a third world country citizen in the '90s with virtually nothing, to where I am today, grateful to possess spiritual and material abundance through no extraordinary skill of my own; imagine where you'd be in five years if you started today.

DR MEHDI ETTEHADULHAGH

Dr Mehdi Ettehadulhagh is truly a man of many hats – from that of a former pro-athlete to a medical doctor to an actor. In addition, he is the podcast host of VOTCAST and a serial entrepreneur who co-founded VOTWEAR, a Norwegian award-winning SmartWear company known for apparel that directly enhances the user's physiology, dubbed invention of 2019 by UMPAC and seen in multiple top-tier publications such as *British GQ* magazine, *Wired*, and *Yahoo Finance*.

In the next decade, Dr Ettehadulhagh plans to focus on making SmartWear clothing an item in everyone's home.

"Gone will be the days where your shirt or socks do not have some sort of tech or 'super power,'" he says, "and with the work ahead of us, one has to rely on consistent and predictable inspiration. Thus, I believe inspiration on demand can be taught."

To learn more, visit: https://votwear.com

Instagram: https://www.instagram.com/mehdiettehadulhagh

Votwear Instagram: https://www.instagram.com/votwear

HOW POSITIVITY LEADS TO SUCCESS

DON SANDEL

What if I told you that your success has very little to do with external forces and your environment, and has everything to do with that wondrous space between your ears?

And it's all based on a simple statement.

The difference between success and failure is your mindset.

That's it – simple yet profound. There is no single factor that can predict your outcomes better than developing and sustaining a positive mindset. Your mind is the genesis of your outcomes and it drives your emotions and behaviours. And if you are successful shifting your brain from a negative default to a positive one, you will discover opportunities that have always been there, but you just couldn't see them.

Years ago, I ran leadership development for a large, global corporation and reported to the global head of HR. She was an extremely bright and influential person, but we had a 180-degree different approach to leadership. As you can imagine, this caused us to butt heads consistently. One day, while she was clearly frustrated with me, she requested that I share my leadership philosophy with the entire global HR team at our next team meeting.

A no-win situation.

On presentation day, we passed in the hallway. As we walked by, she scowled at me and deadpanned: "Well, today's your big day. Don't blow it." (Like I said, different leadership philosophies!)

That's all it took. Herculean self-doubt took hold, and I immediately regretted the impending presentation. My self-talk was so negative that I questioned decades of leadership expertise, numerous awards, a healthy self-confidence and even considered feigning illness. (Nothing too dramatic, just some obscure illness to receive in reply: "Why, yes, by all means, go home immediately.")

But alas, I stayed, an uncharacteristic mass of self-doubt, and delivered perhaps the worst presentation of my life.

As I look back at the experience, I can't fault my boss. My response and my mindset were all on me. But I attribute the lousy outcome to a negative mindset. And the outcome was woefully predictable!

As the Greek Stoic philosopher Epictetus said: "It's not what happens to you, but how you react to it that matters."

I share this story during my workshops and then take a quick poll, asking: "How many of you have experienced something like this? Whether a positive mindset produced positive outcomes or a negative mindset produced negative outcomes?" Thousands of people have answered the question with an astounding 99% positive response.

I would assume, dear reader, that you have as well.

We have all been witness to a mindset that foretells the future. So, our aim should be to create such a mindset that predicts our success.

To get there, we'll first need to understand that 'space between our ears'.

The Neuroscience

The negative mindset described above was more than just an obstacle to delivering a quality presentation. At the moment I allowed self-doubt and a threat to my status creep in, I actually (and your negative brain does this too!) limited the capacity of my brain.

While consciously unaware, our brain becomes focused on the danger that it perceives, whether real or imagined, and the limbic system takes over. This is the emotional centre of our brain, meaning our entire cognitive mechanisms go into Fight, Flight or Freeze mode. When the brain is in this 'threat' mode, its focus is our survival, not our life satisfaction. Blood rushes to the larger muscles, heart rate and blood pressure rise, and the stress hormone cortisol gets released, providing energy to deal with potential danger. Cortisol also suppresses the immune system as well as the 'happy chemicals' dopamine and serotonin, leaving us sick, tired, and ill-tempered. So, the very resources required to be at our peak are diminished to keep us, as our brain sees it, alive! When responding to this threat (the brain doesn't distinguish between a physical or a social threat), we actually limit our physical, psychological, and socio-emotional capabilities.

But it's Not Our Fault

We have a genetic pre-disposition to negativity. We can thank our ancestors for this. Early humankind was always searching for danger, instantly determining if the rustling bushes were friend or foe. It was better to miss lunch, than BE lunch. That allowed our species to live another day but it is also the reason for our negative default. It kept us safe. It keeps us safe. But with an overwhelmingly negative mindset.

According to the National Science Foundation, we have up to 60,000 thoughts per day. Of those thoughts, a shocking 80% turn out to be 'negative' and 95% are duplicated from the day before. Furthermore, a study from Cornell University found that 85% of what we worry about doesn't happen and of the percentage that does happen, 79% of the study subjects discovered that they could handle the challenge better than they expected or that it taught them a lesson worth living. Finally, according to the same study, 97% of our worries are baseless and result from an unrealistic pessimistic outlook.

So, if it's true that our brains move away from threats (and limit our capabilities), it is also true that they move towards rewards (and multiply our capabilities).

In her tome, *Positivity*, Dr Barbara Fredrickson, wrote the following: "But positivity does so much more than simply signal the absence of negativity and health risks. It does more than signal the presence of safety and satisfaction, success and health. The latest scientific evidence tells us that positivity doesn't simply reflect success and health, it can also produce success and health."

So, our challenge is to limit the effects of a negative mindset, and in that vacated space, build a positive mindset.

This is further substantiated by the research of Dr Sonja Lyubomirsky, who completed a meta-analysis of 275 scientific studies involving almost 300,000 subjects. As a result of this rigorous study, Lyubomirsky not only supported Fredrickson's claims, she further showed that those with 'frequent positive affect' tend to produce 'long-term flourishing'. Those who make this positive mind shift also:

- Make more money

- Become better leaders

- Have more fulfilling marriages

- Have more friends

- Are more philanthropic

- Cope better with stress and trauma

- Have healthier, stronger immune systems

- Live longer

- And perform better at work

Simply put, when we have a positive mindset, we are better in every domain of our lives.

Let's further examine how our physiology changes when we have a positive mindset. We simply aren't the same. In other words, we launch a biological transformation in the service of positive outcomes.

If a negative mindset limits our capabilities, then a positive mindset must multiply them. As Shawn Achor writes in his bestseller, *The Happiness Advantage:* "It turns out that our brains are literally hardwired to perform at their best not when they are negative or even neutral, but when they are positive." Our brains change, our guts change, our neurons change, our tissues change, and our chemicals change.

These changes are part of a complex chemical process that enables us to feel emotions: it's based on a chemical reward system that acts as a biological incentive to repeat beneficial behaviours. Here are a few chemicals that play a key role in this positive transformation:

Dopamine (neurotransmitter) – prominent in the body's reward system, this chemical feeds the reward pathway in the brain and is involved in motivation, drive, pleasure and addiction. It gets released when we set a goal, as we progress towards a goal, and when we attain a goal.

Oxytocin (neurotransmitter and a hormone) – often known as the 'love hormone' or 'trust hormone', this chemical helps create human bonds by being released during childbirth, intimacy, the giving of gifts, empathy and kindness, and builds trust when expectations are met.

Serotonin (neurotransmitter) – this chemical regulates sleep, mood, and appetite. Increasing serotonin in the brain is the primary target of most antidepressants. These pharmaceuticals tend to help keep serotonin in the synaptic gap longer, increasing the duration of the feelings of happiness. It gets released during proud moments (and related memories), exercise, and even sunshine.

Endorphins – are produced by the central nervous system to help us reduce pain and boost pleasure. They are three times more potent than morphine. Strenuous exercise, intimacy, crying and laughter all release endorphins. They also increase levels of dopamine.

Note that these positive chemicals are increased by exercise and decreased by stress.

Positive Organisations Benefit Too

But it's not just individuals who benefit from the release of these chemicals, positive mindset, and the resulting increase in wellbeing. Organisations that have a predominantly positive workforce see every relevant business metric improve. As Dr Kim Cameron states in a University of Michigan study: "High levels of effectiveness in organisations have been documented when the positive dominates the negative."

In their HBR article entitled, *Proof That Positive Work Cultures Are More Productive*, Cameron and Dr Emma Seppala further argue "that a positive environment will lead to dramatic benefits for employers, employees, and the bottom-line". Costly factors such as health expenditures, disengagement and turnover are mitigated in positive cultures.

How Do We Get There?

With the case made that a positive mindset is indeed a game-changer, how can individuals and organisations take action?

Individuals

- Savour positive moments. Allow them to exist in the brain longer and be attached to memory.

- Build authentic, positive relationships. One Harvard study states that "relationships are the #1 predictor of health, longevity, and cognitive strength".

- Reframe negative events to the positive. Train your brain to observe your thoughts, reframe to the positive, and see failures and other life challenges as opportunities or learning moments.

Organisations

- Develop a strategic plan to improve both engagement and employee wellbeing. Such a thoughtful, integrated approach will allow employees to bring their best selves each day.

- Create a positive culture. Hire leaders who look to catch people doing things right, not wrong, where positive reinforcement builds relationships and encourages employees to repeat beneficial behaviours.

- Build trust and psychological safety. Both innovation and relationships will bloom when employees feel it is safe to take risks, provide feedback, and even make mistakes.

For both individuals and organisations, creating the environment where positivity can thrive should be a shared goal. By shifting from a negative default to a positive one, we remove physical, cognitive, and emotional barriers that have served as obstacles to our best. If you want to conquer your challenges, be a success and a game-changer, begin with your mindset.

DON SANDEL

Formerly an adjunct professor of English and Communications, Don Sandel has spent the last 30-plus years leading organisation efforts in talent and leadership development.

Don is an expert in leadership development and the impact of shifting to a positive mindset. He is a sought-after speaker on the topic, speaking at national and global conferences, and has been published nationally. Don is the Founder of GoPositiv, a boutique training and consulting firm that makes the link between a positive mindset and engagement, wellbeing and performance. He has consulted for Wintrust Bank, Remarkable Health, Sunovion Pharmaceuticals, Astellas Pharma, Ada S. McKinley Community Services and AstraZeneca and has thrilled thousands with his energetic keynotes on shifting to a positive mindset.

Don volunteers in his community, and is an avid reader, often found reading books about neuroscience, travel and history.

LinkedIn: www.linkedin.com/in/donsandel
Website: www.gopositiv.com
Email: don@gopositiv.com
Facebook Community Group:
GoPositiv Community Group | Facebook

MASTER YOUR MINDSET AND MASTER YOUR LIFE

DAVID BURGESS

You can achieve anything in life, regardless of your current circumstances. In this chapter, I'm going to give you the tools, tips and tricks that I use on a daily basis to overcome my challenges and keep on track with my capabilities.

These are just some of the tools that I also give to my clients. The changes they report back to me are outstanding and some have even said life-changing. They have changed their mood, their relationships, and their financial situation all for the better, by mastering their mind.

I am excited to share these with you today and I know that as long as YOU do them on a DAILY basis and YOU put in the work, you too will see remarkable changes in your life.

We have two sides to our brain. The left brain is the more analytical and methodical in your thinking. If you are like that, then you are a predominantly left-brain thinker. If you tend to be more creative or artistic, you're thought to be right-brained thinking. The brain and mind are very powerful things, as is the body.

The human body sends 11 million bits of information per second to the brain and the conscious mind can only take in 50 bits per second, so the rest is handled by our subconscious. This is the default operating system that handles everything. It's our conscious mind that gets in the way, by throwing seeds of doubt into the mix – taking on other people's limiting beliefs etc. The tools I will share with you will help you recognise the thoughts that stop you from taking action or limit your true potential that we both know you have inside of you. You just haven't been given the keys and tools to be able to unlock that part of your mind. Until now. So, get ready to start!

The truth is, you can change everything when you set your mind to it. I would like to talk about the mind, body and spirit connection. Don't worry for all of you reading this, hearing 'spirit' and automatically your brain was about to switch off as a big warning flashed up saying woo woo alert! I want you to stay with me here.

Thoughts literally become things. Everything you see around you today never existed until someone had to think it into existence. Look at Thomas Edison, the inventor of the light bulb. Everyone said it couldn't be done, it was impossible. From a young age, teachers said he was too stupid to learn anything, and he was fired from his jobs for not being productive. Everyone just thought he was a crazy person. But he kept on thinking of creating a light bulb so that we no longer had to walk round with candles and oil lanterns. He believed that there was another way and he believed it with every ounce of his body. He could create the working light bulb and he was famously asked by a reporter: "How did it feel to fail 1,000 times?" His reply was: "I didn't fail 1,000 times. The light bulb was an invention with 1,000 steps."

He could easily have listened to all the naysayers, the doubters and the insults and taken on board their limiting beliefs, but instead, he chose to ignore what they were saying because he had programmed such a positive mindset that he would create the light bulb and help millions of people to be able to light up the rooms in their homes without having to walk around with lanterns or candles.

The reason I'm sharing this story with you is so that you have more of an understanding of the power of our mind. Edison could easily have quit and thrown in the towel after his first, second or third failed attempt and listened to the criticisms and insults on a daily basis but he didn't quit.

His mental toughness was effective. Look at all the other great people that came before him and after him. Richard Branson, severely dyslexic and one of the most successful businessmen on the planet. Muhammad Ali ("I am the greatest"), Martin Luther King ("I Have a Dream"). All of these greats came from difficult times and bad upbringings. What they all had in common was an amazing mindset and discipline.

I am going to teach you a combination of things and I share these exercises with every single one of my clients. As long as you repeat these exercises daily, you will start to see the shift in your life. Things will start to look a lot easier than harder. You will be jumping out of bed each morning feeling amazing. You will be able to take on anything that comes your way.

The first step is gratitude. Start a gratitude diary. This is my first daily exercise. I want you to go and buy an A5 or A4 notebook and every single morning, I want you to write out 10 things you are grateful for. You can talk about many subjects. Healthy body, work and success, money, relationships, passions, happiness, love, life, nature and the planet, earth, air, water, the sun or material goods. Write about any subjects and start your sentence with: "I am truly grateful for *what?* because *why?*" For example, I am truly grateful for my car because it helps take me and my family safely to my destinations. There are some little rules. You can't write the same thing each day and each day you have to write 10 different things down.

Also find a smooth stone or crystal that can fit nicely in your palm and at night, think of all the things you are grateful for. Hold the stone in your palm and focus on just one of those things out of the 10 for that day. This helps your brain look for the good in things rather than the negative.

You must change the language you say to yourself on a daily basis too. Most of the time we have very damaging words that we repeat to ourselves, like 'I can't do that because of x' or 'I am not good enough' or 'I am too stupid'. Stop yourself in your tracks as soon as you notice your negative self-talk and change it to 'I can do it, I am great' or 'I am learning this new skill with ease'. Change it to a positive programme rather than a negative one and use affirmations. My favourite ones that I use daily are: 'I AM ENOUGH, I AM A MONEY MAGNET, I ATTRACT ALL GOOD THINGS INTO MY LIFE NOW.'

Most of us forget to breathe properly and I have a great breathing exercise which mixed with cold water exposure helps with worry, anxiety and depression and it's all free! The breathing exercise shouldn't be done in any water i.e. bath or open water, or while operating any machinery or while driving.

The first thing that I do and I ask my clients to do is this breathing exercise. When you wake up, place your feet on the floor and say the words 'thank you' three times. Really feel the gratitude of being alive and give thanks. Then lie on your back and breathe deeply into your stomach, expand that first, then move to your chest and let the air out smoothly by just letting go and not forcing the breath out. I do this continuously around 30 to 40 times, that's 30 to 40 breaths in and out. On the final out breath, hold your out breath and use a timer to time how long you can hold your breath on the exhale. This isn't a competition with anyone. Listen to your body; when it really wants to breathe, do it. Repeat the process three times so in total that will be around 120 breaths. You may feel lightheaded or a tingling in your body but that's normal. Do this on an empty stomach first thing in the morning. Because you are giving your body more oxygen, it won't be used to it at first, because we all forget how to breathe properly. We breathe from our chest and not the belly.

This method was developed by Wim Hof aka The Iceman. Look him up, he has a free app. This method has literally helped me with my anxiety, stress and both my physical and mental health. I teach this to my clients.

I then take a cold shower. Please consult your doctor before doing these exercises if you have asthma or a breathing condition and also if you have a heart condition.

Even if you hate the cold, I challenge you to do this for just 30 days and you will notice a huge difference in yourself. Start off by getting into your normal warm shower and when you are ready to turn on the cold, focus on controlling your breath as I demonstrated earlier. Go into the cold water, controlling your breath in and out and stand in the cold shower for just 15 seconds. After 3 days increase it to 25, then gradually increase it to where you are able to stay in the cold shower for one minute. Do this for 30 days and you will have formed a new neural growth in the brain. You'll discover you are capable of so much more.

So, to recap, the best way to start your day is to do these things in this order:

- Wake up, place your feet on the floor and say thank you three times

- Write your 10 things that you are grateful for

- Don't look at your phone or the news first thing

- Meditate for five minutes

- Read a book that is going to stimulate your mind like this one for at least 10 minutes

- Do the Wim Hof breathing method and take a cold shower

- Reframe your negative self-talk with 'I am enough, I can achieve anything'

- Set your own positive affirmations

- Do some form of exercise before you go to work – go for a walk, run or do a workout

I am a dad to two kids under five. We all have the same 24 hours in the day. You can do this. I wake up at 4:30am to get it done. The books I can recommend to help are:

- *Miracle Morning* by Hal Elrod

- *The Magic* by Rhonda Byrne

- *5 second Rule* by Mel Robins

DAVID BURGESS

David Burgess is a professional magician and mindset coach. He has been amazing audiences all over the world with his sleight of hand skills and fun personality, but he was always fascinated by the human mind and how it works.

This led him to want to dive deep into coaching and the mind and how it works. He then decided to take a master coaching course followed by a Neuro Linguistic Programme (NLP), timeline therapy and hypnosis.

He then ventured into coaching others on how they can truly unlock the power of their true potential and their mind and he now helps countless clients realise that anxiety, fear and depression can all be overcome. David helps his clients unlock their true potential.

He is also a father to two beautiful children, Emilia and Caleb, and dedicates this chapter to them and to his wife Rebecca.

Contact David: https://linktr.ee/dbmagician

THE TRUTH IS THE RESISTANCE YOU FEEL INSIDE

VICKY POOLE

When you are learning something new, you practise it to make it right. You know that you have done something correctly when you get the outcome that the book tells you is correct or you receive the approval from those around you. What happens when you get the right answer but you can't help but feel that it is wrong?

Throughout my life I recognised that I avoided certain situations because I felt wrong even though the answer was right. I would be plagued by the memories of previous experiences and my life would constantly replay the same events. Only after I learned to reframe my past did I create the future that I wanted and now I help others to do the same.

My Story

My parents were both born in the 1940s into a time where conflict was the norm. It was perfectly acceptable to declare your views, speak them, shout them or punch them. I was a victim to two parents who mentally and physically abused me until I was in my teens and fought back. With conflict being all that I knew, I sought out conflict at school but I was safely into my 20s before I realised that something wasn't right.

Both sets of grandparents were born in the 1910s, before women had equal rights to anything including our own children. I could never understand why my grandmas would fuss around my grandads so much. The expression 'to keep the men happy' was bounded around the house as a constant reinforcement that no one cared how you were feeling, but if the men were happy then everything was well. As a young girl, I started to believe that no one really cared about me or my opinions and I would find evidence to support this. I was banned from playing football with the boys. I was forced to play the piano because my dad liked it. Even at school, I took subjects that my dad wanted me to study and even went to university to study maths even though I would have loved to study marine biology.

Becoming Mum

Unsurprisingly I wasn't really close to my mum growing up. I doted on my dad and as the only man in my life, only his opinions mattered. Despite having two younger sisters, we never saw them because he disagreed with their life choices and he would impress his disapproval onto them by cutting them out of his life. They seemed to be doing just fine without him though.

I so desperately wanted my own family and yet I had seen history repeat itself with my parents being just like my grandparents.

How was I ever going to find a way to break the cycle of my own past and make my kids so much more than I am today? I first needed to find a partner which in itself had its own complications. I could never find a partner that I really liked, there was always something that I would settle on. They didn't have a high regard for women. They didn't like how much money I earn. They didn't like the fact that I bought a new car. The list went on. Then in a moment of sheer inspiration I wrote out my 'Perfect Man' attributes list because how would I know if I didn't have a list to compare him to?

Dwayne 'The Rock' Johnson's body was at the top of the list. And in fact, I took inspiration from my ex-partners and phrased each attribute positively. I met Martin 30 days later and I've never looked back. Within two years, we were getting married and shortly after that I was pregnant. My dreams were all coming true and yet the moment that I held my son in my arms, I didn't feel love like I thought I would. I felt fear and I needed to protect him: from me.

Something Old, Something New

With being so comfortable in conflict situations, I naturally gravitated to a high-pressure, stress-fuelled work environment: sales. I was very good at holding my nerve when the world was crashing down around my ears and even managed to make some great sales in the process. Even though I was good at my job, I needed out. As a mum I no longer wanted the pressure from an external source; it was impacting my home life and yet everywhere I went, people told me that I was brilliant. Any change is possible when you believe.

I remembered the process in which I found Martin and wondered how far I could go. Then I remembered a story of Christina Harbridge who joined a debt collection company and was horrified by the lack of respect shown for debtors. Once she finished college, she created her own debtors' company and only hired candidates with heart, compassion and who understood that they were going to make a difference. She decided that she would target her clerks on the number of thank you cards which changed their approach. By treating debtors with respect and helpfulness they were able to clear the balance and help each other in the process. Christina saw something that she didn't like, reframed it and made it new again; her practice influenced the whole industry which now includes an 'ability to pay' in financial assessments for debtors.

There is a profile on Clubhouse that boldly states: "If you have received training in digital sales, you have either been trained by me, or someone trained by me." Jeff Walker escaped corporate life and became the primary carer for his family. There was a new gimmick around at the time called 'The Internet' and Jeff realised that this tool was going to change the way in which people and companies would buy. For hundreds of years, people would read a manual and decide if it was for them or not. With this Internet, no one wants to read a manual anymore, they want to learn and be inspired. In his first live launch he took just $1,608. Now he takes in excess of $1million. Companies worldwide have adopted his Seed Launch approach and replicate it for their own products and make significant money every time.

What I learned was that I needed to be targeted in the right way to make it work for me. I wanted to be a brilliant mum but had no idea on how to be. I wanted a fantastic career but didn't want the pressure of everything that I had suffered before. I started a self-awareness journey. I peeled back the behaviours of my upbringing and targeted my core self. When I understood what made me tick, it made implementing it so much easier. I brought Intention to everything I would do.

Conscious Choice

I want to be a size 6 UK and have a perfect bikini body. I also like chocolate, takeout food and chilling out. In everything that we do there is a push or a pull. You can give up smoking or adapt to a healthier lifestyle. When you are pushed from something, it introduces a scarcity mindset. You need to enjoy it while it lasts. It will be gone tomorrow. When you are pulled towards something, it welcomes an abundance mindset. Anything is possible. I never wanted to become my parents. I never wanted my children to suffer at my hands in the same way I did. I was pushing from my past. I set out to change, intentionally and consciously to a 'pull'. I got angry and initially resisted the change because admitting that I needed change was somehow reinforcing that I'm a bad parent, which I'm not. As I sat and saw what was coming up, it was my programming that was resisting. I realise that I can't change that, but instead I can recognise it and consciously choose whether this is something that I want.

One of the beautiful things about being a parent is that no matter how old your child is, they will inevitably do something that you did at a similar age. We as parents repeat what our parents did to us and the cycle will endeavor to repeat. Introduce conscious choice and it opens up all of the possibilities.

I was doing the household jobs one morning and I mentioned the 'P' word around my son: 'park.' That was it, we're going to the park. When his coat and shoes weren't immediately put on, he threw a strop and after a few minutes of failed attempts to sooth him, I found myself repeating my mum's phrases. I caught myself and quickly asked myself: 1) What experience can I relate to as a child? 2) What did my parent(s) do? 3) How did that make me feel? 4) How did I want to feel? and 5) What would my parent(s) need to do to make me feel this? I immediately scooped up George from the floor and hugged him. We sat cross-legged for some time and once he had stopped crying, I explained to him what was going to happen and how he could help. My opinions never mattered as a child and I never had the opportunity to do what I wanted. I wanted my parents to talk to me and explain why something was so. In that moment with George, I consciously gave him the things that I wanted as a child. Love. Respect. Understanding.

Summary

I am blessed to support so many different people make conscious decisions in their life. I love working with parents who want to use simple processes and strategies so their kids can grow up without limitations. Whether you are escaping abuse, trying to break through a career glass ceiling or find your true love, changing your thoughts then implementing them as conscious actions is the key to success. Life is not a spectator sport; you can simply do things that spring to mind without a plan. Or, you can set an intention and consciously choose to do more actions, each of which will take you one step closer to helping you achieve what you want. The actions and choices you make don't have to be based on your past, nor do they need to be perfect every time. It starts by doing them slowly, building your confidence and in time, they will become second nature.

VICKY POOLE

Vicky Poole is an ancestral healer, coach, author and speaker. She was emotionally and physically abused as a child, and was forced to live her life according to other people's expectations, forever disappointing to her family. As a result, Vic has battled stress, depression and anxiety and has come face-to-face with suicide and came through the other side.

Once Vic became a mum, she recognised herself acting like her abusers and knew something needed to change. In her practice, she works with other parents to make conscious choices in their life, to create the future that they want.

Working through her company, Vicky Poole Coaching, she is thrilled to have been invited to be a regular contributor to Sibella Publications from May 2020.

A proud Geordie lass from Newcastle (UK), Vicky now lives in Reading (UK) with her husband, son and two fur babies.

Website: www.vickypoolecoaching.co.uk

Contact Vicky: https://linktr.ee/VickyPoole

SELF-HEALING FOR SUCCESS

Branka van der Linden

Hello Meaningful!

Welcome to this amazing book of sharing. How was your day today? Do you dream of being successful?

Inner Drive

My strength has been depleted, and my life is not what I once thought it was. We all have a degree of faith until things don't go as we expected them to. At that moment, our worlds, as well as our faith, can fall apart. This chapter is not a lesson on intrinsic versus extrinsic motivation.

It is about difficult conversations we need to have with ourselves to change our perspective and move forward in life. When Adam asked me to contribute to this book, I thought hard about how I could bring the most value as a business consultant and corporate trainer. It turned out that the theory can be read in textbooks or by attending one of my webinars, but experiences are unique, so I decided to share my personal story and my journey of self-healing.

Where do I draw my enthusiasm from? Simple things, really. A song that touches me, both melody and lyrics with deep meaning. Sometimes, just gifting a smile to someone without expecting to receive one in return does the trick.

Let's try a short exercise.

Take one deep breath, fill up your lungs and belly. Then hold!

How many seconds did you manage?

Did you concentrate on counting? Or were you just mindful with the intention to complete the task? That is how you can focus your energy on anything you intend to do, including cheering yourself up. Makes sense?

Another secret on how to be successful is to learn how to reduce all the external noises and be in touch with your inner self. You will be amazed how many ideas start flowing through your mind when you are left to just be. We are not human doings.

I am not a particularly good sketch artist, or painter for that matter, but I appreciate art. I could sit for hours looking at the paintings collection, creating imaginary stories, and how it was for the artist to make such a masterpiece. We all carry enormous strength within, and where we channel our powers is where we will get the best results. And for that, we have to break patterns sometimes.

Breaking the Patterns

Have you been thinking about trying to look after yourself but haven't done anything about it?

I was, for the longest time, since I had children (so let's be honest 12 years give or take) and then one ordinary day I received my calling.

I had a troublesome marriage, which I almost successfully ended.

I needed to break away and stay with my thoughts to reconnect with my intuition, so I could find the strength deep within, to forgive, first myself, and then the person who hurt me too.

I was always a very private person. That's how I was raised. Our dirty laundry is not something you broadcast to the world. Oh boy, how wrong was I! I was surprised by my own manifestation powers when I asked the angels to give me a sign, and I woke up to receive that message. The wind blew laundry all over Africa.

So, I changed the game. I put myself first and started rightfully demanding and redeeming 'me time'.

Let's get back for a moment to the story of how I gave myself that necessary time and space.

July 2018, a sunny day in the city of Belgrade, in Serbia, my home country. I participated in the 'Train the Trainer' programme hosted at The House of Vuk's Foundation, intending to excel my career in a different direction. I know how real the struggle is, and the fear of stepping into the unknown. I healed through learning, and you can rise above the water too.

This historical building, of cultural heritage, was a two-storey house in the academic art style of the day, built in 1870. It had this folk ornament motif, and everything seemed like it was made for giants. The hall, stairs, and railings were massive and traditional, only to lead to this bright, modernly equipped minimalistic training classroom.

I still remember it like it was today; they asked us to step out from the modern classroom and come to this traditional foyer with a massive wooden table and choose a card with which we would introduce ourselves to other participants and trainers. Oh, I had that story ready in my head, and then suddenly someone took the card I had set my eyes on, right in front of my nose! So instead, I took the card I liked the least, a yellow flower with the title 'calling'.

When my turn came to introduce myself, all I managed to say was: "I don't know what am I doing exactly, nor why I am here, but it was my 'calling.'

When I came back to Cyprus, I immediately started doing research on those cards and the methodology behind the 'Points of You' brand. I fell in love on the first read, and the rest is history…

Crossroads

I stood strong and resilient. I wish!

That came only later when I learned to embrace change.

In November 2019, I felt the urge to break free, to do inner research. I wanted to attend Points of You Academy without a clue how I would afford it. I committed anyway and had a strong belief that money would come.

"Sky is not the limit and dreaming big is obstructed only by one's own limitations."

Business picked up, and right after I had come back from Dubai and India, I was in a position to secure my academy attendance. I felt relief.

For me attending Points of You Academy and getting skilled in personal and professional development training was a turning point. Or rather the culmination of what I knew subconsciously for quite some time. In February 2020, I packed my bags and went to

Portugal. Turbulent flight from Barcelona to Porto was a story of its own. Did you know that the biggest surfing waves in the world are in Portugal?

While I was travelling to my destination, there was a large conflict in me. My marriage, my relationship, my career path, I was questioning everything. My definition of success is living with no regrets; yet I was heavily regretting not taking my kids to meet their uncle (my half-brother), and the news that he had passed away came as a big shock, a wake-up call. Recovery is a process and if you don't give yourself time to heal, you'll only be making things worse for yourself in the long run.

So, when it feels like you are getting stabbed in the heart, you should look at it and think of it as a physical sports injury, as even when it doesn't look much, the damage below the surface is still there. Social media does not help with a constant stream of messages that we should be better, prettier, richer, faster and more successful. Be gentle to yourself.

Dealing with Change

Changes can be hurtful and not easy to see every time.

Do you ever catch yourself perhaps burning the candle at both ends? How do you heal?

Healing is about nurturing ability to recover from difficult situations and bounce back by adapting to change.

I believe there comes a point in time when we start vibrating at a higher frequency, and we realise that we have changed, that we acknowledge and understand, and most importantly, embrace self-love and self-care. We start aiming for life with no regrets and leaving toxic relationships behind. We also discover this new courage to make bold moves, take more risks and pursue our happiness.

Whenever I host workshops based on 'Points of You' methodology, the feedback I receive from participants is that workshops help them see through the illusion and move through life awake and aware. We use metaphors and powerful language of today's world, the language of photos, that inspire and provoke the mind. So, feeling stuck in your relationship or career is just an illusion. Seeing the big picture is equally important, and magnificent possibilities are out there, but you must reach out with your hand; you need to do the work. I know I did.

All Hands on Deck

Whenever we are going through major changes in our life, we need a support system. The truth is there is something defined as overconfidence, and it can be pretty messy if we don't speak up and ask for help. There is a lot of commotion about work-life balance, and many try to achieve it; some teach it, but rarely anyone talks about their failure. For me, for the longest time, it was a work-life conflict.

Whether on a professional or personal level, the new beginning is like a Lego board with endless dots where you can connect the blocks and start building. Endless combinations and endless possibilities. That is why it is important to learn how to release your imagination. What has helped me the most is crafting and utilising the art of affirmations to find inner peace. Surrounding myself with high achievers and optimistic people gave visible results. I found a new way to create balance and excitement in my life, and this is how I can help you too.

Sometimes you need to make tough decisions, cut your losses and move on. It takes some practise to distinguish the line between prematurely giving up and actually realising it's a dead end. That is where holistic mentors like me come in handy.

And while you may not know what works for you, you can definitely find the magic ingredient by doing extensive research and trying out different ways to heal.

Imagine that you are at the beach, you walk into the sea, and sand covers your feet. What happens in the first moment? Can you see your feet under the water? It takes some time and a lot of standing still for the sand to sink back to the bottom and for the water to become clear again, doesn't it? I believe sometimes you need to take a step back and see things from a different angle. We all have the power to heal ourselves from within.

This way, you can find true courage and confidence in your decisions and take a bold step forward in the direction of your dreams. And the wisest thing I can share here from my personal experience is that dreams change, and that's ok too.

Branka van der Linden

Branka van der Linden originates from Serbia and considers Cyprus her home. While maintaining a strong corporate career, she supports several NGOs. Branka doesn't hesitate to speak up and often quotes Alan K. Simpson: "If you have integrity, nothing else matters. If you don't have integrity, nothing else matters."

Branka developed the CODFISH (Communication, Organisation, Delegation (Fresh Ideas Start Here)) method to help organisations lacking productivity. She is the founder of Meaningful Synergies business consulting and country leader of Points of You.

Branka's holistic approach to business and life purpose earned her honours in 'Women Leaders To Look Up To' in 2021. Not defining herself by her occupation gives her enormous strength to help others any way she can. She is a mentor and published author. When asked to summarise her mission, she refers to her company slogan: 'Empowering zeal & zest.'

Contact Branka: https://linktr.ee/brankavdlinden

TURNING ADVERSITY INTO PROFIT

ALLAN KLEYNHANS

Adversity is part of life. Nobody gets out of this life unscathed by it to some degree. We are all going to encounter it at some point. We would all be better off if we were told by our parents early on in our lives to expect it and more importantly, how to deal with it.

Very few of us are taught the skills of resilience and the benefits of managing adversity effectively and so we spend most of our life trying to avoid it at all costs, without realising that we are missing out on some of life's greatest lessons.

Many of the most accomplished and influential people of our time faced great adversity. How did they turn it around and leverage their pain to create even greater success and fulfilment? The simplest answer is that they processed their painful experiences in an empowering way. We must realise that we have the freedom to choose whether we are empowered by our adversity or not. When things are going awry, the vast majority of people find it difficult to see past their immediate crisis and ask themselves what the deeper learning and value might be.

So, then the question becomes: 'Does adversity always yield value?' The answer is a resounding 'yes'. There is always deeper learning and value available. We all have had painful adversity that has also provided opportunities further down the road. We can all trace our current fortune back to some of our darkest and most painful moments if we look hard enough.

"Every adversity, every failure, every heartache carries with it the seed of an equal or greater benefit." The first time I read this line in Napoleon Hill's classic work, *Think and Grow Rich*, I flat-out refused to believe it. It was July 1988 and I was 21 years of age. I had just returned home from the military after two years of service and I was in a state of shock. I was deployed in Angola for seven months in 1987 and it had taken its toll in a severe manner. I asked myself: "How can going to war be of any benefit to me...?"

Although I refused to believe this line when I first read it, I wrote it out on paper and stuck it on the wall in my bedroom and I contemplated it. What I've come to learn since is that the most powerful lessons are often also the most painful to bear. At some point, we all face adversity and it will either define us or break us. The writer William Ward once said: "Adversity causes some men to break; others to break records." Sadly, for most people, the first part applies, and their suffering is endless and yet completely unnecessary. They miss the gift that lies within their adversity.

What we don't realise is that we are always processing our experiences and our environments through questions and if we don't ask the right ones, we always get the wrong answers.

Everything that happens to us while on the earthly plane, is always supporting our growth and spiritual evolution. We all have a spiritual curriculum here on earth. The significant emotional experiences we have as children that impact and scar us so deeply, can also serve our spiritual transformation as we evolve into fully conscious adults. We can discover who we really are by asking deep questions: 'Who am I and why am I here...? What is my life going to be about and what legacy will I create while I'm here?' If we get stuck in the after-effects of an adversity suffered early on in life and remain focused on what we believe we have lost, we will fail to see anything else available.

So how do you go from feeling that sense of tremendous loss to the understanding that your adversity is quite possibly setting you up for a much bigger win further down the road? You learn to trust life. You lean in and surrender to what's coming up. This is very, very difficult. It's in our nature to survive at all costs and our nervous system is automatically triggered when we perceive any kind of danger. Our ego kicks in and screams loudly at the injustice of life and the things that seem to befall us accidently, without consent or invitation. If we can pause a moment just before our ego begins to protest and ask ourselves in the midst of that small pause, 'what's really going on here?', with an expectation for deeper understanding of the situation we find ourselves in, we open the ability to engage in an empowering conversation with ourselves and arrive at an empowering meaning as a result.

Henry Ford said: "Thinking is the hardest work there is, that's why so few people engage in it." I believe he was referring to conscious critical thinking – deep reflection on the task or problem at hand. This means engaging all of your creative faculties to work on finding a solution or a way forward through your problem, obstacle or adversity.

When we realise we are spiritual, energetic beings having a human experience, we realise our human experiences are merely stepping stones to a higher level of consciousness and understanding of our life here on earth. When we encounter a significant challenge or adversity, our best course of action is to ask ourselves how what we are facing will serve us long term. That answer may not appear initially, especially if the adversity we are facing is traumatic or even tragic. However, that doesn't mean we must refrain from being our own best resource for finding a powerful solution or course of action to turn our adversity into profit.

I believe that nothing ever happens by accident and everything always happens for a much greater reason than we can see or understand in the moment. There are three powerful questions that you can use to approach any problem or adversity you're facing currently or may face at any time in the future. The first is: 'What's really going on here?' This implies that there's more going on than initially meets the eye. We are always deleting information to avoid overwhelm. The brain is always looking to focus only on what it needs to, in order to keep moving us forward in the pursuit of pleasure, while seeking to avoid any pain. When we are ready to keep asking ourselves to observe what else could be going on within us, we free ourselves up to have a breakthrough in our outlook and the way we perceive our experiences and the events around us.

The second question is: 'What's the truth?' This question allows us to be honest with ourselves about what's happening in real time. This avoids the chance of being hijacked by our ego and following the 'wrong' train of thought that would lead down the road of judgment and conflict. The truth will set you free as the saying goes; however, first it will often give you a rude awakening. When we ask this question, we empower ourselves to find the truth of the experience unfolding. This avoids getting stuck in the loop of an internal narrative that keeps us stuck in old paradigms and beliefs.

The third and last of the three questions is: 'What would love do now?' This is my favourite question! For many years I was lost in my own limiting perceptions of myself and the world around me – I hated who I saw in the mirror and consequently hated the world around me. One of my limiting beliefs was 'it's not available to me' – everything I saw wasn't available to me. I suffered under a thick layer of limiting beliefs, all of them vibrating and festering in my unconscious, playing out and creating havoc in my life. Studying quantum physics, religion and the behavioural sciences eventually led me to the powerful subject of spiritual psychology, a subject I absolutely fell in love with! After 22 years of extensive education in this field and the area of unified field theory, I've come to the conviction that we are the creators of our experience and we create our life with the way we process the world around us, through thought, word and deed. This makes us completely responsible for our lives – an idea or thought that terrifies the majority of people.

When you can accept you are the creator of your life experience completely, you empower yourself to address every challenge you face in a resourceful way. When you encounter any adversity addressing what you're facing using the questions I've shared above, along with the understanding you are a spiritual being, or 'energy being', if you prefer, with tremendous creative ability, as well as a spiritual curriculum to fulfil while here on earth, it enables you to transcend any and all obstacles on your way to the ultimate vision you hold for yourself.

I've done exactly this with my own significant and considerable challenges. I was traumatised as a child living next door to a police station for the first six years of my life in a very racist regime. Later, as a soldier, aged 19, I went to war in Angola, a war which raged for more than two decades and was considered the bloodiest war in Africa. After many years of inner work, I only began to seriously change my life and profit from past painful experiences when I began to ask myself the big questions most of us shy away from – 'who am I?' and 'why am I actually here?' 'What's my life going to be about?' 'What will people say about me when I'm no longer here?' 'What will my children say and think about me after I've gone?'

These kinds of questions provoke deep contemplation – take the time to sit and think about these questions deeply and how they relate to your past and your future. When you look at your past, ask yourself: 'What is life teaching me?' Even if you aren't ready to entertain the idea that you're an energetic being having a temporary human experience, focus on the fact that every adversity or challenge has something of equal benefit to offer you in terms of lessons and gifts. We are here to evolve and grow into the infinite potential we possess.

Life is always offering us the opportunity to become more. Each and every experience we have, including even the most dire of adversities, offers us the chance to reframe the experience from suffering into meaning and from meaning we create freedom.

ALLAN KLEYNHANS

Allan Kleynhans is a walking lexicon of human development and potential, having studied psychology, philosophy, the behavioural sciences and consciousness for 33 years and counting. His vast knowledge and expertise as a passionate and highly skilled facilitator on the subjects of human behaviour, communication, self-mastery, conscious leadership and spiritual psychology have helped thousands to make significant personal and professional breakthroughs. He loves helping people transcend the limiting mental constructs of their human psyche to create lives of true fulfilment, outrageous success and authentic self-expression.

Contact Allan: https://linktr.ee/allankleynhans

MATERIALISING THE SKINHQ VISION THROUGH FRANCHISING

HAROON DANIS

I believe any business can be scaled and until a business is scaled you can never really know what the potential of that business is. Some people may be happy with a small business which they can run and simply get by on the income. But I have always wanted to create one which is scalable internationally. I loved the idea that a business starting from a small shop could one day be a national chain, growing internationally into a global brand. I wanted to make a real impression with my brand and travel the world whilst building something of substance and impact, for the benefit of others.

There are so many ways to grow now and there are so many paths you can follow depending on the type of business you have. Whether it's a physical bricks and mortar store or an online business, there are products and logistical solutions almost everywhere in the world. There's so much potential and opportunity depending on the product that you sell. I fulfilled my dream and did it with my business, SkinHQ, which is a skin clinic offering services which help people improve and maintain the health of their skin, from the outside in and from the inside out, without neglecting the mental health aspect of skin health.

We started in a single unit, in Manchester, in June 2017. The seed to what was to become the livelihood for 250 people all started from one little empty clinic, with one guy, a host of ideas, and a laptop on his knees whilst sitting hopeful yet determined, with a plan and an ambition to make this tiny and seemingly unremarkable seed a global company of relevance.

SkinHQ is now on the path of becoming a global brand with 26 locations, in five different countries across three different continents with more than 250 staff. Achieving this within this short space of time took a lot of hard work, a clear vision and sharp focus. Beyond that there was a global pandemic and we had to close for six months with no trade, but through franchising we made this possible and so too can any business owner.

Scaling the Business

After creating SkinHQ, it has now come to reach a certain replicable standard. I realised that every business can be scaled. It's just about finding the best formula to scale your business. The barriers I faced by creating a replicable standard for others to follow allows those followers to learn from my experience, my hardships, and my lessons. I realised that if we are in the same business, pursuing the same goal down the same path, we will all end up stumbling on the same rocks on the path. However, by creating a replicable standard you can light up the path for others, mark out the stumbling blocks and provide a roadmap for the traveller to reach the same level of success you managed to reach. Your sleepless nights and anxious impatience now is someone else's sweet lull and relative certainty. It's all about having a strategy, finding a way to scale your business.

I believe everything can be scaled and it's not just one type of business that is scalable. It's just a matter of finding the right way of scaling your business. For my business I built a formula which I can replicate. I created almost a flat pack system that can be assembled just like furniture. I started in a small clinic in Manchester. Once we found a model that worked in the first clinic, I simply replicated it. Finding the right model took time, but my dream was so big, that every action, campaign, and choice of our products and treatment options was tested and analysed, tweaked, and again tested and analysed to reach that dream. Eventually, the business was booming with glowing reviews and smiles all round.

When you want to replicate something, you need to make it simple and resist the temptation to overcomplicate. We have a lot of competitors, but we picked a few of the products and the services that we felt have the biggest impact and biggest following. We focused on those and didn't overcomplicate. Hence, replicating came like a breeze. The clinics were always fully booked because it was easy for our customers to understand what we do and what we stand for. Through careful consideration of every aspect of our business, we knew how to serve our clients and how much time and training would be required per client. We were able to move fast and be agile. We were flexible and were able to maximise the space that we have. Once we did this in Manchester, we replicated the formula in other cities.

We opened in four cities and realised that we were able to achieve the same success in these cities as we did in Manchester. This, however, was not without certain inherent limitations. It is a business where we needed people to run the business. People who had some risk, a vested interest and skin in the game, who might make a loss if the business did not run right. We felt that the clinic would run better if there was someone present who had some degree of risk involved in the clinic. That's how we realised the crucial and seemingly secret ingredient of how to scale the business.

How I Found My Way

After 18 months, I opened the second clinic in Birmingham, then a third in Bradford, a fourth in Liverpool and my fifth clinic in London. Then I realised that I had another challenge. Since these are physical locations that involved people serving our clientele, the locations that have me, or anyone within my close team, did much better. The reason for this was that there was a sense of personal responsibility over the location and skin in the game. I had something to lose if that location didn't do well. So, I thought to myself, how can I get people to run the clinics that are sufficiently invested in the brand? How could I make people genuinely invested in the brand? There and then was when I realised that franchising is the answer.

Why do I get people to invest in the brand? If I've got people that are financially invested in the brand, then we can work together to try and make it a success. Sometimes if you have someone to work with, you can truly realise your own potential. Let's learn about the intricate things that may be hard to understand through generic software solutions or hard to understand through the little whispers happening within the place - the team dynamics. These are the things that can be managed by someone who's truly invested in the brand. As soon as we had our franchises open, I could see this happening. I've got partners involved in running each of the locations. So, again, it's something that works and now

I can replicate this again. By franchising, we have found a way to run our business in a more streamlined, and more successful way, and in a way, that's better for the business as a whole. This is something that any business owner can do. This is also something that many business investors and potential owners would like to have available.

Where We are Now

My first franchise partner was Robert Svan, who is a psychotherapist with a passion for helping people suffering from anxieties due to poor skin but with limited business experience in the beauty industry. Now, he is investing in his second franchise just a month after opening his first. So, we need and benefit each other. Robert is now making a lot more than he was before getting involved with SkinHQ. With a broader knowledge base to draw from, as we now have medical doctors, dentists, social workers and others from all manner of expertise benefiting and contributing to our brand, SkinHQ is a much more successful business now. We basically found a way of franchising to create a community of people that are all almost equally invested in the success of each location. That's a really powerful thing and ultimately was the formula for the scaling up of SkinHQ that was needed to help us grow at the pace that we're growing now.

Now that we have this chain of clinics in place, we can really make a difference with any treatment that we do. It's like a springboard. It is a national and international launchpad to any treatment that will come out, which allows our positive impact to be that much greater and, to all of us involved, amazingly exciting. I can also focus on my job which is to innovate and bring things to these clinics. I spent some time in Dubai, which is one of the most saturated markets for this industry. I analysed what treatments they have there, and what's missing in the UK and found some next-generation treatments and brought them to the UK and across all our locations internationally.

So, for the franchise partner, everyone does their role within the company and it gives an opportunity for me to bring something into the kind of network that could benefit everyone. It all comes down to speed, like the speed of what ideas are rolling and the speed of scalable growth. That's how we've grown our business; through aiming high, focus and analysis, proving the concept and inviting others to buy into a piece of the pie where they can benefit from our pooled resources and SkinHQ can benefit from our franchise partners' broad experience and dedicated commitment through their individual vested interest.

It took me so long to realise the right way to conduct the business as easily as it is conducted today. These franchise partners are buying into over 10 years of experience of making the right moves and the wrong moves and learning from my mistakes. Now I know exactly how I should operate the business, so it becomes a profit-making business and franchising is all about passing those lessons on. The franchise partners are not just buying a brand, they're buying simplicity. This is the essence of business growth, offer your hard-earned knowledge and experience to others who will pay you to avoid the same mistakes and help you grow faster, safer and with greater agility than you could ever have done on your own.

I am now helping people franchise their own businesses. I share the things I have learned to help them find a way to implement this fantastic business model. By franchising, you can open your business to whole new revenue ecosystems. As we did, you can also benefit from having a community of investors supporting the vision that you focus on.

HAROON DANIS

Haroon Danis is a multi-award-winning disruptive entrepreneur and best-selling published author. His brand SkinHQ has grown internationally and with that growth he won 'Entrepreneur of the Year' in 2020 in the Stevie's International Business Awards as well as the Great British Entrepreneur Awards. SkinHQ also won the coveted Stevie's International Business Award for 'Company of the Year'.

Haroon is an investor, innovator, philanthropist and specialises in scaling businesses. He became an Amazon #1 best-selling author for his contribution to the book *Franchising Freedom*.

For coaching and franchise enquiries email: haroondanis@skinhq. co.uk

Website: www.haroondanis.com

LinkedIn: www.linkedin.com/in/haroondanis

Instagram: www.instagram.com/haroondanis

WHY BEING AN AGGRESSIVE FARMER IS ESSENTIAL FOR BUSINESS SUCCESS

SARAH FRANKLIN

Aggression in Business - Isn't that Bad?

Let me start by explaining what I mean about being aggressive. I don't mean the definition of aggressive of being belligerent or hostile! I mean the definition of being assertive, dynamic, vigorous and bold. Now that that's cleared up, what do I mean about being an aggressive farmer?

Dr Ivan Misner, the founder and chief visionary officer of Business Network International famously stated: "Networking is more about farming than it is about hunting."

In business, pretty much every networking group you attend will say the same. It's about developing relationships with the people around you and building on those relationships so that you can develop trust and credibility. That's all true and a very solid basis to start with.

My issue with this is that it only works if the other people around you have the same attitude and viewpoint and, in my experience, that simply isn't the case.

Spotting the Snollygoster

Sadly, there are a lot of 'hunters' out there in the business world who are only in it for what they can get out of it and have little or no interest in helping you or anyone else achieve their goals. Some of these are more interested in themselves and their business and cannot see the 'bigger picture' of why developing relationships are important. These people can be worked with and may change their attitude. Others, however, are snollygosters who need to be avoided at all cost! A snollygoster is someone guided by personal gain rather than by principles or any need or inclination to assist others. In business, the key is being able to spot these individuals – and as quickly as possible. To do this, being firm and vigorous in holding people accountable for their actions is important and a great way of getting people to show their true colours – and spotting those snollygosters!

A few years back, I remember sitting in a room of about 30 other local networkers where everyone had committed to doing one action to help the others in the room. This was the perfect example of farming in the business sense, as we were all thinking of how we could help each other and the group as a whole. There was, however, one person in the room (who always did very well from the group) who thought it was okay not to do what everyone else had committed to – and, by that point in time, had actually already done. Unfortunately, almost everyone else in the room let this person get away with this without making them accountable for their (lack of) actions. The next time around that this same commitment was asked from the group, it came as no surprise to me that several thought it was also now okay not to do what was asked of them. It was downhill from there. It was bad enough that the individual had let the group down, but by not being held accountable, this had also had the knock-on effect of diminishing the commitment of the majority of the group.

Accountability for Actions is Key

It's so very important to hold others accountable for their actions because, if you don't, you are not helping them, yourself or others around you. You are still 'farming' but doing so in an assertive way!

Completely aside from business, holding people accountable for their actions generally is often important – but sometimes it is a very hard thing to do and certainly outside of our comfort zone.

Quite a few years back, I recall coming out of court. I had won a very hard-fought case against an older, male opponent. My client was delighted with the outcome. As we walked away from the court, I heard my opponent say to his client very loudly in a public area: "She only won that because she's a woman." Sadly, misogyny is not unusual in the law, in many other businesses and in life, but it was the first time I'd heard someone use it so blatantly and openly about me. I had for years heard pit lane 'banter' from other teams saying to their drivers "you can't get beaten by a girl". With motorsport, I knew how to handle it – just go ahead and beat them on the track, but in the business world it threw me. And I did nothing. To this day, I regret having done nothing about it. At the time, I thought I was being the 'bigger man' (pun intended) but I now appreciate that I should have turned around and held my opponent accountable for his comment. Not just for my sake but for every other woman lawyer he was going to come across in the rest of his career.

We are often told in business that being personally accountable is important. That's one of the main reasons we have business coaches – to hold us accountable to do something or achieve a goal. One thing that isn't talked about quite so much though is how important it is to hold others accountable to you. Perhaps this is because it is seen as aggressive – but I am of the firm opinion that, whilst you are developing relationships with others, it is essential to ensure others are accountable for their actions too and that we hold them to account. That way, everyone knows where they stand and the relationship is much more equal. If both parties know that they will fulfil their promises and obligations to each other, that can only strengthen the relationship and make it more successful.

Do What You Say You are Going to Do

If I say I'm going to do something for someone else, it is important that I do it. Otherwise, my credibility will take a bashing. If I don't do it, I would expect that other person to hold me accountable – and I know it is likely to seriously affect the ongoing business relationship we have.

You have to do what you say you will – even if it seems insignificant.

I have often in the racing world helped out other racing drivers either free of charge or at a reduced rate, including giving legal advice and my time, which is, at the end of the day, the way I earn a living and pay the bills. In return, I often just ask for a recommendation on social media and most confirm they are happy to do that. After all, it's not much to ask of them and it helps with my marketing and PR.

Some, however, have failed to just do that one simple thing in return, despite having agreed to do this and having been followed up to do it by me. When they next ask for help, therefore, what do you think my answer will be? Yes, that's right. Full cost this time around! If I don't do that, I'm not holding them accountable for their previous actions and not doing myself any favours either.

This brings me to another point and it's something that has taken me many years in business to learn. If you are going to hold others accountable for their actions, you need to be prepared for them to hold you accountable for yours. Knowing this, knowing your own limitations and that you are going to be held accountable, you have to be careful what you agree to do – and sometimes you have to say no.

The Strength to Say No

Knowing you are accountable for your actions and the impact that this will have on your business if you fail to deliver, should make you think very carefully before committing to do something or take on a job or task.

Holding people accountable isn't always popular but I find it's always better to know how you stand with someone both in business and in life generally – and they tend to know how you stand with them. This is a key to developing long-term, successful relationships.

With my divorce lawyer head on, I see and hear lots of very sad stories every day. Many cases are when one of the couple has decided to do their own thing and the other has simply not held them accountable for it. This drags on and on, often for years until it breaks the relationship and ends in separation and divorce. If there had been some holding to account at the beginning, who knows what may have happened? They could have worked things out or, if not, at least not had to go through months or years of heartache and pain as things drew to their inevitable conclusion.

How Do You Actually Hold Someone Accountable?

There are a number of ways to hold someone accountable and it's important not to let it feel oppressive because this can just cause frustration. Accountability needs to be authentic and done for the right reasons – which in our case is to help develop strong and lasting business relationships.

Remember the 3 Cs:

1. Clarity. The individual needs to know what is expected of them with no room for misinterpretation, including any time frame that there will be;

2. Communication. Depending on the size of the task, continual communication may be needed. It may also be sensible to liaise with them close to the end of the time frame to ensure there are no issues or anything that is stopping them fulfilling what is expected of them;

3. Consequences – good and bad. There is a need to follow up and review. If the task hasn't been fulfilled, discuss what the implications and consequences of that are. If it has, remember to give thanks and praise as appropriate!

You Will Get Results if You Hold People Accountable

Being an 'aggressive farmer', and holding people accountable as part of that is not an easy thing to do and doesn't always make life easy. However, in my experience, any relationships that you do forge like this will be strong and lasting.

People say you only live once. I disagree. You only die once. We live every day. So, be serious about your business and your life. The quality of your life is often about the people around you. Are you surrounded by snollygosters or genuine business colleagues who also want to help you?

I started with a Dr Ivan Misner quote and want to finish with one too. He said: "Don't be afraid to give up the good to go for the great." That takes hard work and holding people accountable is one step towards achieving great relationships in business and in life.

SARAH FRANKLIN

Sarah Franklin has been a lawyer for 30 years, with her own practice for 14, specialising in family law and motorsport law.

Sarah has been racing cars for 15 years, achieving wins in many categories. She is a member of the British Women Racing Drivers' Club and a Brand Ambassador for the British Motorsport Marshals Club.

Sarah is a motivational speaker and commentator, often talking about her life in the male dominated worlds of law and motorsport. Last year, Sarah was shortlisted for the National Law Society 'Sole Practitioner of the Year' award, one of only five people in the country. She is chair of the Kettering Town Centre Partnership and on the Council of the Northamptonshire Law Society. She was named Northamptonshire Law Society Solicitor of the Year.

Away from the worlds of law and motorsport, Sarah enjoys anything Italian, walking with her husband, Adrian, and miniature dachshund, Milo, and learning to play the saxophone.

LinkedIn: https://www.linkedin.com/in/sarah-franklin-55b4206

Website: https://sarahfranklinsolicitors.co.uk

PLAY
THE
GAME

ACCOUNTABILITY FOR YOUR BUSINESS

HILARY HUMPHREY

Accountability is one of those words which can strike fear into the heart. It's the big brother to responsibility. You will be responsible to your clients for delivering your product or service, but you are ultimately accountable for your business and everything that goes on in it. The buck stops with you.

The truth is that you need to take time out to work on your business. It's so easy to get caught up in delivering to clients and finding new clients, that you take your focus off how your business is really doing and what action you need to be taking. If you are looking to grow your business, then being accountable at an early stage will help you to be a really good leader. When people are accountable for their own decisions, work and results, the effectiveness of an organisation increases greatly.

Being accountable for your business covers a number of things. It's not just about paying the bills. Where are you against your goals?

Do your goals tie in with your vision and mission statements? Do you have a clear plan for the year? What is your financial situation? Do you know where you want to be in five or ten years' time?

Being actively accountable also means that you can identify changes in your industry or clients' needs much earlier on. This means that you can make changes to your products or services quicker. This will help you build a sustainable business and reduce the likelihood of you being left behind as markets and clients' needs change.

With a plan in place, you know where you want to be and by when. From here you can break the yearly plan down into the 'how'. Identify the tasks that need to be completed in each quarter and then into those for each month. Don't give yourself more than five tasks in a month. Less if you have some big tasks, such as a website review. Be realistic with the amount of time you have but commit to putting time aside. These plans are no use if you don't take time to take action on them. Reviewing where you are is the next step in being accountable. But accountable for what?

Financials. This is the only area I insist my clients review and be accountable for each month. One of the main reasons for being in business is usually to make money. Don't rely on what you see in your bank account though to indicate how well your business is doing. Make sure you know how much you have invoiced for each month and how much your expenses are. You should know how much profit you make from each of your products and services. If you are working hard but not much money is coming in, then is your product or service priced correctly? Or do you have bad debtors to deal with? Bad cash flow management is one of the main reasons businesses fail. If keeping up on your finances is not a task you enjoy, then outsource it to a bookkeeper and ask them to send you a monthly report.

I had a yoga teacher come to me for help as she had no idea if her business was making any money. In the 10 years she had been running her business she had only ever completed her accounts once a year for her tax return. So literally a high-level total of what came in and what went out. She had never looked at the financial side of her business in any detail. I asked her to go through her accounts and identify what each payment was for. By the end of this exercise, she could see which of her classes were best sellers, which were not making much profit and what her expenses were. The task of doing this each month has helped her identify where her marketing efforts need to be, review her pricing and look for alternatives where her costs were high.

The rest of your areas of accountability may vary from month to month depending on what your plans are. You will probably find that they are linked in some way: marketing, admin, client satisfaction, product development, changes in your industry and changes in legislation. If you have a limited company then you need to ensure you are complying with your duties as a director.

If you have come from a corporate background, you will be used to having regular meetings with your line manager, or project meetings. At these meetings you would have been held accountable for tasks set for you. When you work for yourself, this doesn't happen. You now need to be that line manager and take time out, not only to do the actions, but to review them. How do you do this? Make time in your diary to get your business tasks done on a weekly basis and then monthly, take time out to review your business as a whole. Look at each of your tasks you had to do. Which ones have been completed? Which haven't been started or gone to plan? What are the reasons for this? Has anything changed which means that these tasks are no longer required? If you don't like the task, but need to do it, can you outsource it? Are some tasks seemingly taking a long time? If so, can technology help or can you outsource the tasks? Are there any tasks you can stop doing altogether? It's ok to stop doing things that add no value, and this includes selling some products or services.

You need to be very realistic with your answers. And you may not like some of the answers.

Letting go of tasks can be very difficult for the solopreneur who wants to do everything themselves. There will come a time when they can't do everything. Identify the tasks you don't like doing and outsource them if you can't find a way to automate them. And remember you need to keep those that you outsource accountable for delivering. You need to know if the outsourcing is adding value to your business.

How can you make yourself accountable? Organisation is key to this. You could use a notebook and write down all the tasks you need to do from your monthly goal check. You could automate and use software such as Asana or Trello to keep tabs of all your tasks. You can use a planning diary. The key is to finding something that works for you – that you enjoy using and doesn't take a lot of time to set up and use. And be realistic. Not all of these items will be business actions – they could be last minute client requests. When you do your monthly planning think about the tasks that need to be done and when they need to be done by. Some tasks may be a higher priority or need to be completed before another action can be started. Don't look at doing them all in the same week. Spread them out throughout the month, and make time in your diary to do them. This will help reduce the feeling of overwhelm that comes when circumstances change and you head is full of worry over the things you haven't done.

Also have a think about when you are most productive and book your time around this. I know I am better at the more mundane admin tasks first thing in the morning. Come mid afternoon, my mind has fully warmed up and I can tackle those bigger jobs that require more thinking or concentration. It doesn't mean I can't do the bigger tasks in the morning, I'm just much more effective at completing them in the afternoon.

Make accountability fun. Yes, I did just put accountability and fun in the same sentence. Put aside time to complete tasks and review your business. Get out of your office and go to a favourite café and complete your review there. Your favourite drink, a tasty treat and change of scenery can all help you switch off from daily tasks and interruptions. You may prefer to go for a walk first to review in your head how things have gone, before sitting down to look at the facts and figures. Award yourself with a glass of something sparkling when you have done well. Make your review meetings something to look forward to. That way doing the tasks that keep your business running will also feel less of a drag.

If you find it hard to do this on your own, then look for an accountability partner. Some networking groups offer group accountability sessions. You may know someone who is having the same issues, so why not offer to buddy with them? How frequently you want to meet is up to you. You may want weekly sessions with only one task per week. Fortnightly may help keep you on track. Monthly sessions give you a good amount of time between meetings to get the tasks done. You should put aside a minimum of two hours per month and three to four hours at the end of each quarter to complete a more thorough review. Or you can find a business or accountability coach to help keep you on track. Working on a one-to-one basis with a coach will give you more time to focus on your business and identify the action you need to take. It also gives more scope to explore the issues you are facing and challenges you more on why you may not be making progress.

Being accountable will keep you focused on your business goals, the progress you are making to achieve them and changes that you need to make on the way. There is no easy fix for it. You need to put the time in to work on, and review, your business. You need to be realistic with your answers. If you don't think you can do this effectively then you need to find an accountability partner to work with and challenge you. And always remember to award yourself for meeting your goals and milestones. You have worked hard for this.

HILARY HUMPHREY

Hilary Humphrey is a successful business owner who is passionate about supporting business owners to achieve their goals. Running Cardinal Support Services, she aims to support sole traders to maintain focus on running their business, as well as delivering their product or service. Working for yourself can be lonely and sometimes overwhelming.

Hilary has a background in customer service, quality assurance and process improvement, gained whilst working for a FTSE 100 company. She uses this knowledge and skill to understand the individual, their business and their business's market to come up with practical solutions to completing everyday business tasks and ensuring the tasks get done.

Hilary lives in Sussex with her partner and Shru the cat, who is often seen joining in zoom calls. If you would like a one-to-one with Hilary email hilary@cardinalservices.co.uk.

www.cardinalservices.co.uk

CONNECTION ALCHEMY

HEATHER MARGARET BARRIE

In early March 2020, I experienced Fika in Sweden for the first time. A time in every day to share coffee, cake and conversation, Fika is part of everyday life. As a coffee entrepreneur, I had wanted to bring this concept to UK businesses, to make it part of our working lives as a way to improve relationships, spark creativity and enhance mental wellbeing in the workplace (as well as sell more coffee of course!). Lockdown shelved that idea as my corporate office clients closed their doors but I realised that those elements of Fika could be the basis for a new way of supporting solopreneurs to learn and grow in a more collaborative and less isolated way.

I believe that a great business that delivers your version of success is built on relationships and on building relational capital. Human capital, relational capital and structural capital are the fundamental building blocks of an organisation – they are all guided by values and are key to our competitive advantage. But I believe that of these three, even for solopreneurs, relational capital is fundamental to creating a business that is true to your own vision, mission and goals, both personal and business.

Relationships are at the core of a successful entrepreneurial organisation – relationships with prospects, clients, freelancers, business partners and our support structures – the list goes on. Relationships might start in networking, through introductions or via social media and are crucial to how we develop as solopreneurs. As a connection alchemist, I facilitate the start and the growth of relationships amongst our members and I have also realised how relationships are at the heart of growing the business that I run with Richard!

I met Richard seven years ago when a mutual friend thought we might work well together. Even though our characters are very different, our values and ideas are aligned and our skills are complementary. Lockdown delivered an unexpected opportunity for us to work together as Covid restrictions saw the rise of Zoom calls across borders and we realised that our combined networks and LinkedIn connections were peppered with people who could be each other's clients or collaborators or supporters. We created a name, used Canva to create a logo and Eventbrite enabled us to bring our first online event together. We invited 80 people and 39 of them paid us five pounds! Most of that was lost to VAT and fees but our first event, based around networking and LinkedIn engagement was a moderate success! Since then, we've built our virtual business café through fostering relationships, being agile and responsive and learning from our growing community.

It quickly became obvious that the energy and support within the community was inspiring and enabling people to do far more than just network. My working relationship with Richard and our informal, welcoming style had created and built the virtual café and I was beginning to see the impact of relational capital amongst our members. We immediately realised the exponential power of making networking more than just a pitchfest. Our community grew through building relationships and creating a supportive and active learning environment. We had stumbled across a fundamental gap in the market – businesses fitting into neither startup nor scaleup, and who lack the resources or confidence to invest in high-end coaching. They want to grow and need input and support from others in order to achieve that growth. The café's mission had evolved!

You might recognise this scenario. It's Sunday night and like that productivity guru taught you, you've planned the week and set your goals. Your online diary is full – again! Yet by Friday, the to-do list is still long and your targets aren't met and deep down, you know it'll be the same again next week! I've started to reflect each Friday when I don't achieve the outcomes that I had planned. Part of that involves looking at the return on investment of networking time. Did I follow up, did I explore that collaboration opportunity, did I engage effectively on social media? Did I take the necessary action to achieve those goals?

Planning your networking, following up and reflecting on those returns are all important to building quality relationships and enabling growth. So now that you've linked with everyone in every Zoom chat and have over 5000 connections on LinkedIn, you might then wonder who Miranda Smith is when you get notified that she has a new job! Maybe it's time to focus on being more selective with where you network and the quality and authenticity of the relationships that you build to improve the return on all those hours on Zoom!

Our name reflects what we do. 'My Business LINCS Café.' LINCS stands for: LEARNING, IMPACT, NETWORKING, COLLABORATION, and SUPPORT. Our members focus their time online to learn core skills, define their impactful message, grow their networks effectively, create collaborations and lean into the support of a community to enable them to achieve their goals. And the thread that runs through these five core elements is RELATIONSHIPS.

It's great to keep LEARNING – a new perspective, a new way of doing something or just something interesting that helps you grow by integrating it into your business – to be done by you or to be delegated! Learning can be through seminars or from the collective experience of others – Sasha (note these are not their real names) learned invaluable lessons around pricing in one of our growth summits, enabling her to successfully pitch and price a project 10 times higher than her original thinking! Where there is good relational capital, there is always someone (or someone they know!) who can bring different perspectives to our issues based on their skills and creativity.

Your IMPACT is in your message and the ripples of influence you create through being in this world, by being passionate about the challenges you solve and the communities with which you engage. Nadia spent hours on Facebook and Insta without generating many new clients. Following a Q&A session with the LINCS community, she refined her LinkedIn profile, defined her message for an audience with a budget and created a simple and effective campaign on the right platform. She now has an engaged and growing client base who understand her values and the value that she brings to their lives.

Are you overwhelmed by 40 people staring back at you on a NETWORKING Zoom call with the same pitches every week? By the fourth pitch, you can't remember who does what for whom! You've put your Calendly and LinkedIn links into the chat and now you have a meeting next Tuesday with Jilly – who was she again? Networking is seldom about selling to the people in the (Zoom) room – it's about meeting new folk, deepening existing connections and understanding what lies behind the pitch that you've heard so often. Follow up effectively to build those relationships so that people can work with you or share your message effectively – six degrees of separation and all that!

Andy had been to endless networking events since redundancy led to unexpected self-employment as a virtual assistant – she struggled to stand out in a suddenly crowded marketplace. But in our more relational environment, she's learned to focus on the challenges she solves, the results she creates and her credibility. She has focused on developing 'know, like and trust' within the community, who can now share her content and talk about her services with confidence – she has since gained two new clients in her preferred target market!

COLLABORATION and COMMUNITY are essential for business success! In a recent poll on LinkedIn, more than 60% of respondents cited collaboration as the key to their successful transition and growth during the pandemic. Collaborations are ad hoc and formal partnerships that enable us to deliver something greater than we can do alone and can enhance the shift from the 'isolated' solopreneur to the 'interactive and connected' entrepreneur!

Jaimie came to one of our early events – he wasn't sure that his networking objective of meeting corporate CEOs would be met, but was open to the experience. In a breakout room, Rachel described how she works with entrepreneurs who want their writing to be eloquent and effectively presented to enable them to communicate their message. As JB had been working on a book project for a while, he immediately tuned in to the outcomes that RD focused on and a connection was made. A successful meeting ensued and not only is the book now published but this first project has grown into an ongoing collaboration that is key to both of their businesses. A standard pitch in a busy room would have been unlikely to unearth this unexpected partnership!

SUPPORT comes in various forms – mentoring, masterminding, accountability, coaching, social learning, action learning – all ways in which we come together and support each other. Support is vital for existing solopreneurs as well as people who have moved from corporate to business ownership (by choice or by circumstance) and who are suddenly without a team, working alone and from home. Being part of a community and its inherent support structure contributes to a healthy mind and a healthy business. There's no specific anecdote for this – just the messages from members who have found recent times dramatic and isolating, saying repeatedly that being part of a game-changing community has enabled them to survive Covid and to feel supported to thrive into the future.

The truth is that everyone's version of a successful business looks and feels different. In the last year building relationships, collaborating, learning and contributing has enabled many of our members to transform from uncertain solopreneurs into entrepreneurs with successes under their belts! There's a big gap between starting your business, declaring yourself a solopreneur business owner and what you consider to be your successful entrepreneurial self – and you don't want to feel that being a solopreneur is a solo journey!

We call ourselves a café because sharing conversation and commerce over a coffee is as important today as it was in the coffee houses of the 17th and 18th centuries and even if much of life is online these days, connections and collaborations will always be key to our success. Grab a coffee (or tea!), reach out and connect with someone for Fika. Be bold and embrace the randomness of life, for your success will be based on the connections and relationships that you make in unexpected places and the lessons that you learn along the way.

HEATHER MARGARET BARRIE

Heather Margaret Barrie is a connection alchemist and award-winning coffee entrepreneur. 20 years in accountancy wasn't fulfilling her dreams, so she set up a mobile coffee bar in 2005 when she discovered her passion for coffee!

As a natural communicator and connector, Heather missed interacting with her regulars when the bar closed in 2017. Then she discovered Swedish Fika – the daily ritual of taking time out for coffee, cake and conversation. She has woven these Fika principles into a thriving online business partnership – My Business LINCS Café.

Heather hosts regular events at LINCS which inspire creativity, collaboration and relationships within a community of entrepreneurs who want to learn, connect and grow.

Heather has twice been named Business Personality of the Year and has twice run for parliament. She is a passionate cook, gym-goer, podcaster, cyclist, sea swimmer and lapsed bridge player!

Contact Heather: https://linktr.ee/heatherbarrie

THE POWER OF SPEAKING THE SAME LANGUAGE

MICHAEL ROBISON

There is a strange power and leverage in the ability to speak and be understood. It is something we often take for granted. In fact, many of us neglect to put much thought into the magic that occurs when we are speaking the language. It opens doors, creates synergy, removes barriers, and allows us to achieve goals. It is a crucial ingredient in building healthy, thriving and effective teams.

If you have ever travelled to a new country or region where the language is different, you can reflect on the frustrations that occur when trying to communicate the most basic needs or ideas. It can be difficult to simply acquire food, directions and make meaningful connections. And, in many cases, it leads to frustration and confusion. Those negative emotions and moments can often cast a shadow on an experience that would otherwise be more fulfilling and enjoyable.

This is most often the case for leaders, entrepreneurs and visionaries in their own journeys. As they are working to build support, teams and companies, they often experience great frustrations. These frustrations feel like impossible barriers, or roadblocks to being successful. They can leave leaders disheartened, demotivated and feeling weak.

Have you experienced these sorts of feelings as a leader? Have you felt a sense of frustration and weakness? Imagine being able to overcome these challenges and feelings. What would it mean to you if you could unlock the power of speaking the same language with your partners, your team and the people in your life?

For most leaders, executives, entrepreneurs and visionaries who experience the frustrations that come from these sorts of barriers and challenges, the assumption is they have the wrong team. They often feel as though they have hired the wrong people, or in many cases inherited an ill-equipped team. However, this is almost never the case. In the end, the frustrations and struggles often lie within the inability to communicate and be understood from both sides.

In the pages ahead you will learn the skills to open a more meaningful way of communicating, helping your team communicate and both parties being understood. This is a crucial step in building teams that have the power to change the future, impact the world and thrive. With these tools, you will find that teams who speak the same language are able to overcome obstacles and become a force of nature.

Let's establish something very important about each one of us. There are three areas of life from which we all operate. These three areas drive our decision-making, our manner of communication and our mode of operation. When we recognise these in our lives and the lives of those around us, we can establish a common ground of understanding and communication. These three areas of life exist for every person, regardless of their career, identity or position in life. It is a common place from which we can all align ourselves and choose empathy and understanding.

The Three Areas of Life from Which We Operate

The first area of life from which we operate is our personal values. Our personal values drive our core decision-making. They inform us of our pattern of ethics, of right and wrong, and cause us to judge the concept of fairness. These personal values are transferred to us from the ways in which we are raised, and shaped by our experiences in life. As children, many of our values are transferred to us from our families and friends. We adopt the values of our families and friends, most accurately those values which have produced positive experiences and fair outcomes in our lives. Yet, as we become independent, and we encounter success and failure in our journey, our values are informed and shaped.

Your personal values can be both positive and negative, and they may even seem obvious. Most of your personal values will be easy for you to share, but there are always those unspoken values, like unspoken expectations, that seem natural to you, but values that others may not clearly see. Learning to express these values in full is a first step in creating the power of speaking the same language and being understood.

So, what are your personal values? It is time for a little homework. Take out a sheet of paper, and number a list from one to 12. In each spot list a simple word or statement that describes your top 12 values. This will seem to begin easily; however, as you approach the last few, you will need to think, to dig deep into your person, in order to complete the list. Your values may include things such as loyalty, forgiveness, courage, education, efficiency, security, and adventure. This list is about you, it is yours uniquely, and there is no wrong word or statement to add to your list. Once you have completed your list, set it aside and let's move on to the next area of life.

The second area of life from which we operate and exist is our business practices. Don't be mistaken, even if you are not a businessperson by career, we all interact in business transactions daily. Every interaction in our lives is a business transaction. There is a give and take. Even by introducing yourself, you expect a response, a basic transaction of give and take. As with personal values, many of these business practices are transferred from important people in our lives, and then shaped by our own life experiences.

We each have a specific set of ways in which we transact with the world around us. I have even seen this play out in my children. Their mother has taught them the importance of finding a deal, or extracting maximum value for every dollar they spend. A few years ago, while on vacation, I gave my children a handful of dollars to spend as they pleased in a special market. Each of my kids took their time to discover the item(s) they would choose. At the end, my youngest looked at me and asked to make a trip to a local thrift shop. When I asked why, he said he could get more toys for his dollars in another place. Even at five years old, he had already adopted the business practice of finding quantity over quality. He was happier with something previously owned, than having something brand-new. He has adopted a business practice opposite of my own, but very important to his mother. This is something each one of us has experienced in our lives. As we mature, we adopt and engage new and modified versions of such business practices.

Now, like before, grab a separate sheet of paper and number it one to 12. Take some time to write down your top 12 business practices.

Again, this list is uniquely yours, and there is no wrong answer or statement that can be chosen. Your list may include things such as efficiency, value, fairness, service, memorable, relational, etc. You may find similar statements or words on this list as on your first list, and that is perfectly okay. Once you have completed your list, let's move on to the final area of life.

The third, and final, area of life from which we operate is our passions. Our passions are the very things that drive us from within. They are the things that wake us each day with vigor and excitement. They are the things that fuel our dreams and visions. Our passions are the fire within our soul that brings satisfaction and contentment when experienced. Some of our passions are transferred, but the vast majority are shaped by our experiences in life and things we desire, but have not acquired or accomplished fully.

This is often the easiest list for you to complete. Again, on a separate sheet of paper, number a list one to 12, and take time to write down your top 12 passions. Your list may include things such as travel, family, romance, affluence, security, learning, and much more. Again, you may find similar statements or words on this list as on your first list, and that is perfectly okay. Once you have completed this list, it is time to create some magic.

The magic is found in creating alignment in your life. You can align your personal values, your business practices and your passions. When you align these three areas, you honour yourself and create a space of fulfilment and contentment.

Creating Alignment and Magic

Now, let's create some alignment here. Take your lists, lay them out side by side. Reflect on the items in each list. You are looking at 36 words or statements that best describe yourself. These are the very things that 'make you tick' and inform and shape your decision-making, leadership and lifestyle. This is a small reflection of the person you have become.

Your next step is to look for similarities in each list. Look for common themes and ideas. The objective here is to look for a common idea that represents three core focuses in life. The first is a common statement that speaks to what you want from your life. The second is a common statement that speaks to what you hope to give to others, the people around you. And, the final is a statement of the legacy you hope to leave behind.

I will give a personal example here. In my values list, I have the words 'education' and 'learning'. In my business practices, I have the words 'risk' and 'new ideas'. In my passions list, I have the words 'travel' and 'adventure'. When I look at these words, I see a common statement or word that encompasses all three areas of life. I am able to take this common thread of words and statements and encompass them into one word, and align all three key areas of life into my statement of what I want for myself out of life. That word is 'discovery'. I want to live a life of discovery. I want to discover new knowledge, experiences, businesses and cultures. When I pursue this, speak to this, make decisions around this and share this with others, I am on a path to fulfilment for the things I want for my own life.

If you follow this same method for your statement of what you want for others and for the legacy you want to leave, you are on a path to fulfilment, contentment and power. You are honouring yourself. And, when you are able to share this with the people around you, the people you lead and the people you want to inspire, you will find something magical. All of a sudden you are understood. People can understand why you make the decisions you make, why you operate as you do and your purpose behind each word and action.

Now, let's put this into action for your team. Lead your team through this same exercise. Help them learn to communicate what matters most to them, about them and for them. All of a sudden you can find alignment, strength, respect and understanding within your team, relationships and more.

This is when you and your team begin to speak the same language. And, this is when a leader, an idea and a team become unstoppable. This is a game-changer for your life, your team, your company and your legacy!

MICHAEL ROBISON

Michael Robison is a strategic business consultant, leadership expert, investor and advisor. He was named one of the Top Leaders of 2021 by Yahoo! Finance and one of the Top 10 Influencers of 2021 by Huffington Post. Michael has nearly 20 years' experience in senior leadership and growth-focused organisations. He has served as a CEO, tech startup founder and non-profit executive director.

Michael has owned multiple bricks and mortar luxury retail chains and has been the head of a prestigious FinTech startup. Michael and his team at D5 Group created the Alignment Blueprint – the secret weapon strategies they have delivered to some of the top brands, companies and leaders in the world. Additionally, Michael is a trusted contributor to Nasdaq, CNN, BBC, NBC and Yahoo! Finance.

Michael lives in Franklin, Tennessee, with his husband, Cameron. They have seven kids, five of whom are still at home.

LinkedIn: https://www.linkedin.com/in/michaelrobisond5

Instagram: https://instagram.com/misterclubhouse

PLAY
THE
GAME

GAME-CHANGING BRANDS

DARRELL WAYNE IRWIN

It's easy to lose your way in business because of a lack of clarity. Clarity brings currency. Currency to trade with, currency in terms of reputation and obviously currency in the bank. The four Bs of brand which give any business clarity are belief, belong, best and beyond.

I help people build the business they've always wanted with a purposeful brand. I have found that brands with purpose outperform those without. When you put cause before cash, and impact ahead of income you attract the right attention.

A clear and purposeful brand will create empathy and provide a gateway to add value. My four Bs tried and tested methodology is about how you can best communicate your offering through your brand and how telling your story in the optimal way will supercharge advocacy.

When you tell the right story, you will get the right enquiry. To be unique in the marketplace, the product or service needs to be good but the real strategy lies in a clear story.

BELIEF - Mission, Vision and Values

The first 'B' to address is belief. Belief in you. Why does your business exist? Many businesses don't know what they stand for even though they have a call to action. We want to help you create a cause to action, a mission.

Mission is your cause to action – it should never change! So, mapping it out for you, it flows like this:

C	Call	Using (How you answer it)
A	Ability	The Media (What is your superpower?)
U	Utilise	To Create (How do you act?)
S	Solution	Community Impact (What legacy is)
E	Execute	Globally (Where in the world?)

A story starts with a belief, an assignment, a mission. (NB Mission and vision often get confused. Mission is the 'why' and vision is the end game.) A mission is the reason why you exist.

Vision that Inspires Decision

Vision is the picture you would paint if money was no option. It's the end game. How do we construct a memorable vision statement?

LEADING POSITION: A World Class (What Influence?)

UNIQUE: Sustainable Creative Agency (The Difference)

GROWTH: Helping One Hundred Thousand CEOs
(Number and Audience)

COMPETITION: Create Purposeful Brands
(Problem Solved/Pain)

RESULT: That Give Companies Legacy
(Best Possible Outcome)

Vision is what attracts people for the longer term as it's the thing that inspires us.

Values Make You Valuable

Holding a set of values that are built around service actually holds you to account. Values help unify the people that have bought into your mission and vision. Values bring the sense of unity and create a culture of success. Values really help us build culture, keep it on track and attract more of the right kind of clients. You can celebrate people who live out the values of the company. Likewise, you can hold people to account against values. Having the right values in place helps you find the right people and keep them. We value people and we back it up with the four-day work week. As a result, we had a whole lot of people wanting to work with us.

BELONG - We All Want a Tribe to Thrive In

Some brands have ceased being movements and have become monuments because they failed to listen to what the audience needed.

The brands that are changing the world are being built around community. Facebook groups, Clubhouse rooms, and even summits are giving people a voice that could not be heard in the past.

Your job is to embrace feedback, not run from it. Without feedback, you'll become a throwback. Don't join the list of companies that didn't embrace the future, like Blockbuster (didn't adopt streaming), and Kodak (ignored digital).

We need to understand where our audiences are at in terms of:

- Demographics – Age? Location? Education? Family? Job title?

- Goals in life – What do they want to achieve? Own a home etc.

- Interests – Where do they spend their time, talent and treasure?

- Motivations – What promise are they looking to fulfil? Like being financially free.

- Frustrations – What is holding them back? Roadblocks, lack of time, money, resources?

We also need to know a bit about generations. The difference between them. Never before have we had baby boomers, Generation X, Generation Y and Z working together at one time.

Generational psychology is worth looking into as a valuable tool in our brand marketing armoury. It's certainly worth knowing that if a Generation X had a £5,000 bonus to spend, the chances are they would buy a new car, watch, computer or sofa, whereas a millennial would be more likely to spend it on a trip around the world. A Generation X would value material goods and prestige and a millennial would value experiences. Another example of how the different generations think is the war between the baby boomers (OK boomer) and the millennials (Snowflakes). It's well-documented and played out most recently in the US elections.

People tend to believe that each generation somehow supersedes its predecessor but it isn't the case. Each generation has a unique role to play.

Let me tell you a story. My grandfather James Irwin was 18 and flying a Seafire (the naval equivalent of a Spitfire) from Malta to the Ark Royal (located 25 miles from Gibraltar) on the 13th November 1941. Three Messerschmitts appeared out of the sun and attacked him and his comrades. One bullet went through the floor of my grandad's plane, up through the base of his chin and out the top of his head. Still alive, he broke both ankles escaping from the cockpit and the plane crashed into the sea. He parachuted into the water from where he was rescued miraculously. At the same time, HMS Ark Royal (the ship James was supposed to land on) was being sunk by a German U-Boat. James had narrowly missed death twice in one day.

James found himself being nursed back to health by an Italian lady, Joy, who became his wife. They began a new chapter. Among their children was Ian Irwin, my father. Leaving home at 16, Ian James Irwin joined the Royal Navy and took on the eighth most dangerous job in the world as a Navy Leading Aircraft Handler, landing planes until just after I was born.

I tell you this because I have been inspired (not threatened) by previous generations' attitude and appetite for risk.

BEST - Your Strategy is in Your Story

Establishing a clear narrative of what makes you the best in your sphere requires a clear value proposition. The simplest route to creating it is by using this statement:

The product/service solves this problem for these people with this system that creates these results in this time frame.

Cre8ion's example: "We build brands that inspire belief and create belonging, to become the best in their sector and go beyond expectations."

Having a value proposition is sharing what's in it for those that you serve and then sharing that story with others. It aids credibility in a language we all understand. Once you have the value proposition in place, you need to communicate it to your suspects (those who don't know you) and prospects (those that know a little bit about you).

Testimonials which frame your value proposition can be crafted around what we call the 'Hollywood Narrative'. Most Hollywood stories follow this Hollywood Arc which plays out in numerous locations: space, the desert, jungle, underwater or in the past, present or future.

Welcome to the Hollywood Narrative

1. Characters – Make the company the hero in this story; they want to do great things.

2. A common goal – The characters have a goal, a desire, a plan to change the sector they are in.

3. The adversary – This doesn't have to be a person, it's the pain, the blockage, the enemy.

4. The plan – Tell the story of the plan they thought would help them win.

5. Attempts and failures – Be real, they tried and failed, they need help, share the failure.

6. Regroup – From 'all is lost' to the moment they discover your business.

7. New plan, same goal – They apply the techniques, the insights, your methodology!

8. Victory – Share the results and where that company is now.

BEYOND - Let Your Word Create Your World

Legacy is what sets you apart from other businesses. Starting with the end in mind is a great way to build a business around a positive legacy. That's why having a vision is so important as it signposts you to the 'beyond'.

Research and development are great ways of building for the future, using 'Trees' (existing business), 'Plants' (two to three-year enhancements to existing business) and 'Seeds' (anticipating the future using technology).

Adopting the B-Corp approach to doing business, for purpose and profit. This is fast becoming the 'fair trade' for business and one we believe in.

Both of these things take time and are well worth adopting for your message, but to start with, you can adopt three or four of the UN's 17 sustainable goals to help you establish purpose.

We worked with a company that had an international presence who produced recyclable plastic trays for ready meals. They needed to address their reputation to show that they were taking the environment seriously. We produced a sales presentation for them clearly showing this commitment to sustainability.

We clarified their mission, vision and values and then did something that was game-changing for them as a business. We aligned their positive activities with three of the UN's 'Sustainable Development Goals'. The upshot of this was that they secured a further long-term contract (they had just come to the end of it) using the presentation we had prepared for them. The clincher for the deal was that their client had themselves committed to exactly the same UN SDGs and when they saw the presentation slide matching their own goals, they made a unanimous decision to remain with our client as their supplier.

Larger companies are addressing their sustainable goal responsibilities by cleaning up their supply chain and that includes you. If you put these into your business now, you'll have a better chance of making the cut or being discovered!

The Four Bs of Brand

These four pillars are belief, belong, best and beyond. Companies that build businesses in this manner create exceptional, lasting impact. Remember the best people and best businesses are focused on impact over income. If they make the right impact the income takes care of itself.

DARRELL WAYNE IRWIN

Darrell Wayne Irwin walked away from co-owning an award-winning marketing agency, and stopped working with certain blue chip brands that sent people to an early grave. Darrell decided to help companies who had a purposeful, life-affirming message instead.

Darrell launched a creative agency, Cre8ion, in a charitable setup. Taking a small team of inexperienced volunteers, Darrell built a brand marketing team to serve both the charity and community and, by 2016, Cre8ion had outgrown charitable status.

Relaunching alone as a startup, www.cre8ion.co.uk built (and still build) purposeful brands using the 'Purpose Playbook Methodology'. Darrell also co-founded a software startup, www.di9ital.co.uk, with one of Cre8ion's founding team. These two businesses remain closely aligned and collaborate on designing great products framed with exceptional brand solutions.

In a 30-year career Darrell has transformed his focus from income to impact.

Contact Darrell: https://linktr.ee/darrelli

SALES SUCCESS SECRET LINK: WHAT THE GURUS ARE HIDING FROM YOU

KAREL VERMEULEN

My Story

What comes to mind when you hear the word 'sales'? What emotions are you feeling when you hear this dreadful word 'sales'?

As a successful entrepreneur, published author and business owner of multiple businesses, one would assume that I love and excel in everything that has to do with sales. Wrong! As a matter of fact, I hated sales. Whenever I had to jump on a sales call or tell someone about my product and service, I would get so nervous that I could hardly get a word out. I experienced all the fear symptoms: dry mouth, shaking knees, forgetfulness, doubt, low self-esteem, frustration, hate, and anxiety. Have you ever experienced any of these symptoms?

In December 2018, I decided that enough was enough. I couldn't carry on like this. I needed to conquer my fear of sales if I wanted to be more confident, inspired, valued, respected and successful. So, to cut a long story short, I enrolled into a 'Sales University' as well as onto every sales course and sales training that I could lay my hands on. It was then that I discovered and learned about this simple, yet extremely effective, sales secret, a 'missing link' that has not only taken one of my businesses out of the red by increasing my sales revenue over 300%, but also raised my confidence, excitement, and energy. I am now operating from a place of calm and peace.

What would it mean to you, your business, and your family if you could have whatever you desired without feeling guilty, stressed, anxious, frustrated, overwhelmed, bitter, nervous, humiliated, resentful and even depressed?

The Secret Missing Link

This chapter is not about all the different sales methods, strategies, techniques and sales talks that you get to learn about whenever you enrol onto a sales course. It is not about how to handle objections, read your client's body language, how to persuade your client into the sale and definitely not about what to say and what not to say.

All the above are important for business growth, do not get me wrong. What I am about to share with you, I honestly believe and have experienced myself, is the ultimate crucial non-negotiable foundation for any success in your business and your life. It is what we call one of the ultimate universal truths that once you grasp, understand and practice this 'secret missing link' on a daily basis, your life will never be the same! It is like the law of attraction. No matter who you are or where you are from, as long as you live within the boundaries of Mother Earth, you will be bound by its law and truth, the law of gravity. What goes up must come down.

The main reason that you do not have what you want, and in the context of this chapter, your lack of sales income revenue in your business, is the fact that you are not showing up as you should to manifest what you genuinely want and desire. It is important to know and understand that there are two worlds we are living in. We call them the metaphysical and the physical worlds. The metaphysical is about mindset and energy; it is who you truly are inside. It is your identity when you are showing up. It is not visible with your physical eyes neither are you able to touch it. On the other spectrum, we have the physical world of which we are all familiar with. It is what you can see and touch, the actions that you take to generate money etc. When you merge both worlds together that is when the magic happens: the manifestation of something incredible that you create. Yes, it is important to learn how to sell, how to communicate to your ideal client and how to market in order to grow your business. The secret 'missing link' is the metaphysical stuff that the majority of people do not focus on.

With the metaphysical, we need to realise that everything is a feeling and we need to feel those feelings right now every single day through the power of visualisation. The secret to true manifestation is to act as if it already happened. Acting as if you have it already. Like faith. Like the law of attraction. You speak it out, live it, and feel it as if it has already manifested. Do not wait for it. You've got to be it. It is the internal work that we need to do first. Most salespeople focus on the outward stuff first and neglect the internal work and this is where most people are getting it so wrong. What you focus on internally WILL manifest eventually externally. One of my favorite affirmations that has helped me tremendously is: 'My thoughts, my words and my actions are powerful forces of attraction.'

The important question to ask yourself is: 'How can I activate the metaphysical world to manifest what I truly want?' You do it by following and practicing these three easy steps:

Step 1: Get Clarity

Get crystal clear on exactly what it is that you want. Clarity leads to certainty and certainty equals knowing. Certainty removes all doubt, and it attracts. Know that your dreams will happen because that is one of the secrets of manifesting. Example: if you want more sales, then how many clients do you need to have in order to bring in the money that you want?

Step 2: Name the Emotions

Determine the exact emotions behind your clarity. Behind everything that we want is a corresponding feeling, an emotion. Money is an emotion. If I have money in my bank account, I feel secure, I feel comfortable, I feel confident and successful. What is the emotion behind what you want?

Step 3: Visualisation

Visualise every day what you want. You cannot do it for a few days and then expect it to materialise. It takes about six to eight weeks for the visualisation to materialise in the physical world. Imagine what you want and how it feels when you have it, even if you do not believe it at first. Speak those feelings and pictures out aloud. Own it by grabbing those pictures and in your mind's eye wrapping it all over your body.

It is important to do the inner work first. The metaphysical work such as this will magnify your life and sales in so many ways. Be mindful of your left brain as it will get in your way telling you it is not real, that it is a coincidence that it has manifested etc. Do the process and the work and you will be amazed with your results.

Your Relationship with Money

I will do you a disfavour if I do not ask you this important question. What is your relationship with money? In other words, what do you think and what are the emotions that surface when you think about money? What is your identity with money?

Increasing your sales will ultimately result in an increase of revenue, moolah, money. Earlier, I mentioned that money is also energy, a feeling. Did you know that how you think about money and the type of emotions that you have towards money can either block or aid you in having the money/income that you want and deserve? Do you feel that you are doing all the work and for some reason your money just does not come in?

'Money does not grow on trees.' 'Money is the root of all evil.' 'Money is scarce.' 'We have to work hard for our money.' 'I do not deserve to be rich.' 'It is better to be poor than to be rich.' Do any or all of these statements sound familiar? These are what we call limiting beliefs and will prevent you from the income that you deserve.

Some people are also afraid of money, afraid of real success and this is blocking them to accept and manifest the true wealth that the universe wants to bestow on them.

Remember, what we think, we attract. And if you have a limiting belief around money (a bad money relationship), then that is what you are going to attract in your life, no matter how many sales courses you take and regardless of all the other inner work that you do. What does this all mean? It means that you have to reinvent YOU around money and understand and appreciate that money is another form of energy. It has a value assigned to it. When you go to the supermarket, you exchange money (paper) that holds a certain value for things you are buying. You have something of value in yourself, your business, your product, and service. You are valuable. It is about rebuilding you. People who make money and lots of money emphatically understand and believe that they are valuable.

This is where it begins. When you rebuild your relationship around money, you are also rebuilding your identity around money. This does take time. You have to invest in yourself, bet on yourself and back yourself up with your new-found belief through constant positive money affirmations and visualisation exercises. Work on your self-worth, your self-esteem, and your confidence. You owe it to yourself, your family, and your clients. It is crucial that you be honest with yourself about what your true relationship with money is. You have the power to change. You deserve to have the best. Ok, how do you change your bad relationship with money?

Step 1: Acknowledge that you have a bad/negative relationship with money.

Step 2: Forgive yourself.

Step 3: Create positive affirmations around money.

Step 4: Visualise your new relationship with money and feel the corresponding emotions.

Step 5: Be grateful for the wealth and income that is coming your way and that you deserve.

On a scale from 1-10, where 1 is exceptionally low and 10 extremely high, how serious are you about turning your lack of sales success into profit?

Do whatever it takes. Take massive action today to get rid of all doubt and negative self-belief habits. You deserve to thrive in your business, to be proud of yourself, feel confident, successful, powerful, respected, valued, amazed, and inspired.

I believe in you. Now is the time to believe and invest in yourself!

KAREL VERMEULEN

Karel Vermeulen is a COMENSA international accredited business coach, successful business owner, and published author. He is passionate about inspiring people across the globe as he believes that everyone is 100% responsible for their own success and that life happens through you not against you.

He is the first South African author to be published by New York publisher Morgan James with his book *Do You Really Want to be an Entrepreneur?* and also co-authored the book *Finding Your Moment of Clarity.*

Karel created the KV brand and is also the founder of Success Growth Academy, an online learning business and personal development platform with his renowned 'Sales to Profit Mastery' and 'Management by Responsibility' (MBR) online courses.

A native South African, Karel currently lives in Cape Town with his life-long partner, their two Jack Russell dogs and his love of tropical fish.

Website: www.thekvbrand.com

Success Growth Academy website:www.successgrowthacademy.com

INTELLECTUAL PROPERTY: YOUR MOST VALUABLE BUSINESS ASSET

STEPHEN CARTER

Innovate or Die!

As an entrepreneur you will be familiar with the idea that you must always be innovating if you want to grow and add value to your business. Innovation allows us to respond to changing customer demands, changes in the environment in which we operate and evolving technologies. It is innovation that helps us confidently stay ahead of the competition rather than running to keep up. Without innovation, a business will plateau and, ultimately, fail.

But what is innovation, really? How does it create value? And how do we ensure that we capture and take full advantage of that value?

To answer these questions, we must dive into the world of 'intellectual property'.

If you are innovating, you are creating assets: new product designs, ingenious technical advances, software code, new brands created for your products, services or business as a whole, a 'five-step formula' that you develop to help your clients succeed. The list goes on and will be unique to each business. These assets, often intangible, are your intellectual property, your 'IP'.

It is in this IP, this collection of assets representing the output from your innovation activity, where the real value lies. If you are to capture the value you must capture and protect the IP.

Try this as an exercise. Note down the different ways in which your business generates or will generate revenue. For each revenue stream, write a list of the distinctive features of the associated product or service – focus in particular on those that are unique to your business. The list you have just written is your first draft of an 'IP Asset Register', listing the key IP assets that underpin the value in your business.

Protect the value

Intellectual property rights, 'IPRs', are legal rights that offer protection for the underlying IP assets.

Strong 'registered rights' are obtained through an application process. Patents protect technical advances, 'inventions', as we like to call them. Registered designs, referred to as 'design patents' in some countries, offer protection for the appearance of new products, for example their shape or surface decoration. Registered trademarks protect elements of brands: logos, names, even colours, smells and sounds in some jurisdictions – think of the 'Moonpig. com' jingle – I challenge you not to be singing that in your head right now!

Other IPRs, such as copyright and database rights come into existence automatically when the underlying IP asset is created. Trade secrets can be a particularly powerful form of unregistered IP protection in cases where the underlying IP asset can be kept under wraps. The classic example, often cited, is the Coca-Cola recipe.

Innovative activity will very often lead to the generation of multiple IP assets of different types that can be protected with a corresponding mosaic of IPRs. Take the example of Speedo swimming trunks. As well as the Speedo brand, protected with registered trademarks, there could be design protection for the shape of the trunks, if new, and one or more technical advances in the material of the trunks that lend themselves to patent protection. There may also be trade secrets associated with the manufacturing process.

Take the list of key IP assets you have created for your business and note down next to each asset whether there is already any IP protection in place. What gaps are there in the protection that might need plugging?

Do you own 'your' IP?

This may seem like a silly question. "Of course I do!" I hear you say.

You would be surprised how often this is not the case.

In my experience, problems with IP ownership are one of the most common issues uncovered when your IP is forensically examined.

Worse still, IP ownership problems are like a ticking time bomb. They do not generally reveal themselves in the normal course of business. Rather they choose the most inopportune moments to explode into view, during due diligence for an investment or sale of the business, or in litigation for example.

The problems tend to arise for two main reasons.

Firstly, people make too many assumptions, without checking the facts. The one I encounter all of the time is the assumption that because you have paid for something you must own it. Sounds reasonable, doesn't it? Unfortunately, when it comes to IP, it is an assumption that does not always hold true.

Take the example of a business developing a new app. They engage a freelance programmer to write the code and a design agency to come up with the brand and the user interface. Without the right agreements in place, the business could find themselves in the position where the programmer owns the code and the design agency owns all of the collateral created for the brand and graphic user interface (GUI).

The second reason comes down to timing. Specifically, confusion or a lack of thought about who created what, when and, most importantly, what their relationship was with your business when they created 'your' IP assets.

For example, especially for startups, it can quite often be the case that key IP assets are created before the company that will exploit them has been incorporated. In that scenario, the company simply cannot be the original owner of the assets and a transfer into the company is required; something that can generally be sorted out easily and inexpensively early on but could be troublesome further down the line.

The rules around IP ownership are not straightforward. They differ by type of IP asset and by jurisdiction. If you want to ensure your business owns the key IP assets on which its success depends, you need to examine the relationships your business has with everyone involved in developing the assets and be certain that appropriate agreements are in place.

Looking back at your list of IP assets, do you know who created each asset, when it was created and what the creator's relationship was with your business at the time?

Your Competitors Have IP Too!

I know that many small businesses favour the ostrich approach, burying their head in the sand when it comes to thinking about the risks that you might face from a competitor's IP. However, it really is much better to face the risks head on so you can work out how to mitigate them before it is too late.

One scenario that I have seen all too often is when a business chooses a new brand without first checking that their adoption of the brand will not tread on anyone else's IP toes.

A relatively simple, cost effective check can identify potential issues before you commit to a new brand. Investing a small amount up front on this check can avoid the embarrassment and expense of a rebrand if, in the worst-case scenario, you launch only to find out that your new brand infringes someone else's registered trade mark. Think of it as 'insurance'.

What about the case where you are investing serious money in developing a new product? If you pay attention to your competitors' IP during the design of the product, you give yourself the opportunity to steer the design around their IP rights. The alternative is to carry on ignoring the IP rights of others, launch your product and then find you are stopped in your tracks by a court action!

So, do you bury your head in the sand or keep your eyes wide open so you can see and avoid the obstacles along the way? It is not always so black and white but if I was considering investing in your business, I know which approach I would prefer you were taking.

Who are your main competitors? Do you know what IP rights they hold?

Be Proactive, Not Reactive

No one is suggesting it is easy to manage your IP. In fact, it is hard. The rules and procedures are complex and working with IP lawyers is expensive.

As a consequence, most small businesses adopt a reactive approach. They consider IP only when faced with a problem or where an opportunity slaps them in the face. When someone else, typically an investor, insists they pay it some attention, there is a flurry of activity and then IP is forgotten again. Businesses operating in this way find themselves reinventing the wheel over and over.

There is a better way!

Be proactive. Seek out the opportunities and face the risks head on. Do this with a plan in place. A plan that sets out your preferred path through the IP maze and guides your decisions around IP ownership, the management of IP risk and your approach to IP protection. In other words, an IP strategy.

The strategy does not need to be complex. It should be something that you, your employees and partners can understand and implement in the day-to-day operations of the business. It should be a living document that evolves and pivots with your business as it grows.

The development and implementation of the strategy requires effort up front but a well-designed and implemented IP strategy will save you time, money and stress in the long-run and help you achieve your business goals.

Pull together your list of key IP assets. Record the details of the relationships between your business and everyone involved in the creation and use of your IP. Take the time to find out what IP your closest competitors hold. Do this and you will have the initial building blocks for your IP strategy.

Put IP at the Heart of Your Business

The truth is that most small businesses could dramatically improve their chances of success by paying more attention to their intellectual property.

You can avoid heartache down the line if you have the right mindset towards IP and get your IP foundations in place at the earliest opportunity.

This does not have to be an expensive exercise. It is quite possible that the 'right' decision for a young business will be to do little more than ensure they own the IP assets on which their business will be built and keep those assets secret in the short term. However, you need to give yourself the chance to reach this decision, rather than ignoring IP entirely or thinking it is one of those things to put on the to-do list for the future.

Think about it now. Recognise the value of IP to your business. And nurture it to set yourself up for success.

STEPHEN CARTER

Stephen Carter is known as 'The IP Strategist'; he is a UK and European patent attorney and founder of The Intellectual Property Works. In the last 25 years he has worked with some incredible businesses, including writing the patent applications for the Speedo swimsuit that helped Michael Phelps to his record-breaking eight gold medal haul at the Beijing Olympics.

Stephen is recognised by 'IAM Strategy 300' as one of the world's leading IP strategists and is now focused on working with ambitious startups and SMEs to protect their innovations using IP strategies aligned with their business goals, helping them to succeed so they can make a positive impact in the world.

Outside of work, Stephen loves Crossfit, spending time with his family, and is a Bath Rugby supporter as well as being Treasurer of his local rugby club.

Website: www.theintellectualpropertyworks.co.uk

LinkedIn: https://www.linkedin.com/in/stephenjcarter

Contact Stephen: https://linktr.ee/theipstrategist

PLAY
THE
GAME

THREE WAYS TO CREATE BUSINESS VALUE USING HR

STEFAN TONNON

After a 25-year career in Human Resources, I have come to the age where I can say it has been an extensive exciting journey and a great learning experience. During this journey, I have been passionate about how strategically-aligned HR practices and programmes can positively impact the business. However, most senior executives still see HR as a cost centre while many HR leaders desperately try to have a seat at the senior executive table. In discussions with other HR colleagues in my network, I often see how frustrated HR leaders are for not having a seat at the table, seeking desperately to make an impact and be a recognised function. In my opinion, it should not be about the seat, as we should instead focus on driving business impact. Only then will you be seen as a business-critical function and a thought leader, and the seat will automatically come with it.

I want to share my journey and some of the decisions I have made throughout my career that can be helpful for your journey ahead in an ever-changing world. The approach I took is to focus on people as we are in the people business, after all. When I talk about people, I focus on the Human factor, the Company, the Market (HCM) and share the lessons I learned.

Human Culture and Values

One of the critical success factors in high-performing organisations is that they put their people first. I fully agree with this statement, and therefore the HR leader should ensure companies are designed, organised, and have the right people culture to enable this. We have all been in situations where we visit a company and see posters in the reception with a list of colourful statements of the company's values. If they have more than three to four values listed, ask yourself how many employees can remember them, let alone live by them.

Therefore, one of the first actions an HR leader should do is focus on defining the business's values and driving its culture and behaviours. Suppose you want to have a people-first business approach. In that case, you need to provide a safe, diverse, and inclusive environment where employees can innovate, be successful, and understand their role in the business's overall success. HR is not responsible for the culture. Culture flourishes in collaboration with employees, the different manager layers and senior executives. The senior executives in the business need to own it, hold their leaders accountable for it, and, most importantly, lead by example.

The start of building a workplace with solid values and an inclusive culture should be done with the end in mind first, your market promise and strategy, and then work backwards to the values and right behaviours that would drive this.

One of the first things I tell HR colleagues is to listen to employees, managers and leaders and see if they align and have the same ideas on how to be successful as a company and know how to contribute as an individual.

I have been in situations where the management team has clear ideas on becoming a one-billion-dollar company in the next 36 months. There were plans discussed, mind map sessions done, market analyses prepared, and after many important off-site meetings, there were cheers around the conference table – mission accomplished.

However, it became challenging to translate those plans into specific directional projects supported by middle management and, even more crucially, the employees. Having 'town hall' meetings and a set number of emails sent out will not bring the troops into action.

This is when HR needs to partner with the top management and build business-wide programmes and actions to create clarity through top executives, the management layers, and employees. To do so, you will skilfully have to translate the strategic business agenda into actionable items forming the fundamentals of a purpose-led and successful organisation. In my opinion, you, as an HR leader, should have been part of the business strategy meeting from the start.

Ultimately, it would be best to convince the business that their most critical success factor is people. One of the CEOs I have been working with during my career has a great philosophy: 'Customers first but people always', which I fully agree with.

The Skill to Understand Your Company Turning Them into Business Gains

Over the past 18 months, with the pandemic and coming out of it, the world has changed. HR professionals have been at the forefront of the discussions, and there is an excellent opportunity to keep the momentum going. When you look at HR in general, they handle policies, employee relations, employee health, pay salaries, deal with talent management, learning and development, only to mention a few traditional areas. To focus on the business outcomes, you need to embrace a broader concept, and I would like to share what I think strategic and business outcomes-driven HR can look like.

As much as you keep your people at the forefront, it would help if you took an outside-in perspective. That means understanding the market forces, trends shaping the future, the business strategy, market potential, competitors, and the impact these have on your HR strategy. Make sure you have one, together with a roadmap outlining the priorities required to execute the business strategy. The roadmap should entail the unique competitive advantage the organisation will have when leveraging its human capital to achieve its objectives and address potential business risks.

Your internal customer, legal, finance, customer support, sales, want you to thoroughly understand their pain points, what keeps them awake at night and how their business is operating. I have always ensured participation in the sales revenue calls, thereby helping me understand how the business runs from a sales perspective, who our customers are, how we sell, and how the customer deals and the revenue streams work. Because of this, it has been easier to provide the proper support at the right time. As an example, you might notice the sales team finds it challenging selling those important complex solutions deals. You and the team could then lean in and work on sales enablement programmes to upskill sales and create bigger deals, increasing deal size, revenue and even a better sales margin.

Understanding the financial reporting aspects and applying your analytical mindset to ensure you can support the organisation with cost savings or investments is another critical capability. Apart from working closely with your finance department, make sure you challenge your team on the investments made in HR. I always ask questions such as: 'What is the business value? Do we have a return on investment (ROI), and if so, what is it, and to what business objective will it be aligned?' You cannot do this without tracking and analysing your HR and employee data. The trick here is to not only analyse the data within the silo of HR but use it in combination with your other business data or external benchmarks. For example, if you were to build a sales enablement team, you would want to understand the best format for the sales team to take the training, what topics and subjects to include, time frames, and how you envisage they apply the learning. You do not want to stop there as you need to align it to the business output, which means tracking if they sell more, deal closure time and other variables to course correct when needed and measure the business output.

The partnership you forge with your internal customers will allow you to discover skills or competence gaps, conduct workforce or talent management planning and prepare for the future skills required in the different departments to enable the business to grow and transform to fit for the future. These are all highly business-critical items.

Becoming a Thought Leader in Your Space Helps Drive Customer Success in the Market

Let us look at the outside-in perspective, which I mentioned and the external business customers.

Most organisations I have worked for are in the technology space, naturally meaning a well-structured sales organisation, a research and development (R&D) or product development team, marketing, and a good understanding of the customers and the market space.

To understand how you can support the business strategy, I recommend any HR leader participate in the sales and marketing events. Whilst there, do not just talk to your sales team; connect with the customers to find out their pain points and challenges. By doing this, I have received invitations to speak and connect with their HR leaders for knowledge sharing, allowing me to understand our customers better, applying the knowledge back into our sales methodology and sales skills assessment.

I have been fortunate to have been asked to talk at a customer event sharing how technology adoption has enabled us, as a company during the pandemic, to mostly work from home. I shared our story with 75 potential customers, and due to my story, we were able to follow up with some exciting opportunities, which hopefully will lead to successful sales outcomes.

Let the People be Your Business Drivers

Your people are critical for driving the company and its financial results and should be your top priority.

Empowered motivated employees results in better business performance. Wellbeing, the ability to integrate work and private life, upskill and progress their career will improve your employee retention.

You should invest in your leaders, providing them with the knowledge and tools to help them use the right behaviours to manage and empower their teams, creating high-performing teams and making them magnet hubs where talent wants to work.

Make sure you develop and build a culture of trust and psychological safety. Creating a diverse and inclusive company where empathy, curiosity and trust are not just words but something your senior executives, your managers, and everyone lives by.

Throughout my career, I have applied HCM but differently to how you might expect. The most significant investment you can make is in people, but do not stop there. If you want to make a business impact and add value as a thought leader, I recommend using the HCM method. It does not stand for Human Capital Management. It stands for a technique that has been proven successful throughout my career:

Human + Company + Market = successful business outcomes and financial gains.

Apply all three together with the most significant focus on people, and you will be a business-critical function and a thought leader.

STEFAN TONNON

Stefan Tonnon has over 25 years of experience in the IT sector across EMEA, US, India and APAC. Stefan worked in executive Human Resources leadership roles in technology companies such as Insight, Infor Global Solutions, Progress Software and Riverbed.

Stefan's passion for people development, diversity and inclusion, technology and sustainable transformational change is the driving force behind his career. He is also a mentor and business advisor for Collective Brains. He is an investor, farmer and ambassador for a startup called Threefold and provides business advice to small tech startups.

Stefan is Dutch and currently resides in Sweden and has lived and worked in the US, Germany, Netherlands and the UK. Being a global citizen has enabled him to understand multicultural, diverse and inclusive environments, which is crucial to driving financial success in international companies and startups.

LinkedIn: https://www.linkedin.com/in/stonnon

Collective Brains:
https://collectivebrains.com/user/stefan-tonnon

PLAY
THE
GAME

ELEVATING YOUR LEADERSHIP FOR A BETTER WORLD

CHRIS COOPER

Are you contributing to positive change or adding to the world's problems?

Are you developing the quality of your thoughts and behaviours so you can make a higher quality contribution? Helping leave a legacy through your life and work by contributing to issues that matter such as climate and nature regeneration, poverty alleviation, equality and justice through leading organisations and noble projects?

Since records began, a minority have used their position and access to the world's resources to increase their power and financial benefit. Unless you believe that acquiring and burying excessive wealth like an ancient Egyptian will help you in any afterlife then wouldn't it be better to ensure you are genuinely contributing to a better world?

Let me share the five stages of the 'Elevating Leadership Model' created with my good friend and leadership thought leader, Gene Early. It is a simple, yet deep perspective, based on over 70 years of combined leadership experience and research.

1. It Starts with You

At age 28, I was at a personal crossroads – no partner and little money. In my moment of need, I discovered a deep interest in self-development and my life transformed.

The realisation that I was the source of my own success or failure required deep personal reflection. Discovering life purpose, vision and elevating the quality of your behaviours over a few years can lead to massive transformation. I discovered that our life stories often give us clues to our path.

I grew up in Scunthorpe, a steel manufacturing town in Northern England. Expectations were not too high. "Chris, why go to college when you can get a job at the steelworks," my grandfather once said!

One day, aged 14, I attended a steelworks open evening with my father. As molten metal lit up the factory like a hell on earth, his stories of 'another one was crushed under the works' train today' played on my mind. Dark, noisy, dirty, dangerous and too many unkind working practices for my liking! After the tour ended, a tall important-looking man walked over. "Hello young man. When you're older are you going to work for us?" "Erm ...you must be joking!"

Unsurprisingly there was a very uncomfortable silence in the car home, until: "Did you know who that was? Only the chief executive of British Steel!! Why on earth did you say that? You might need a job there one day." I sat quietly reflecting. "But Dad – you've never liked working there – why would I?"

I admired and loved my father, yet his 40 years of stressful graft in the steel industry inspired me to leave town to study and ultimately help others become better leaders, employees and create engaging workplaces.

Reflecting on pivotal stories in your life can give clues to your path. Two activities I would recommend are:

Discovering your purpose. Take some paper out right now and answer the following questions:

What would I love to see more of in the world?

What role will I play in contributing to this better world?

Turn this into a short statement that describes what you feel is your purpose and consider what this means for your contribution to your family and friends, your work, your community, your health and wellbeing.

2. Humility

Have you ever met someone whose humility deeply moves you?

Ego might bring confidence to push forward. Humility though is another level. It doesn't mean losing drive, rather adopting values such as kindness, respect, caring and love. Being grounded, vulnerable, open, honest with the ability to listen generously. People with great humility are fully present with you and their energy has a special magnetic influence.

I remember interviewing Marshall Thurber whom after our radio interview asked me lots of questions. I was flattered that such an accomplished man was so interested in me and I asked him:

"What has made the biggest difference to your success, Marshall?"
"Be more interested than interesting," was the reply.

This may have come from Dale Carnegie's *How to Win Friends and Influence People* yet I was extremely impressed by how Marshall embodied it.

The next time you have a conversation, ask a minimum of five questions before you share your opinion. What did you learn and how do you think the other person felt?

You might also build humility by developing your own meditation practice. Deepen what you have or begin with a short, but regular 10-15 minutes per day.

Increase your humility and you will win friends, influence and produce a grounded magnetism that attracts people and new opportunities into your world.

3. Seek the Truth

So, what is truth? Getting underneath to what is true or discovering the root cause of a problem or situation is a worthy pursuit. Truth requires you to thoughtfully consider your life experience, assumptions based on that experience, and what others tell you.

Are you aware of how your deep attitudes towards, for example, race, gender, equality, religion, weight, appearance, even tattoos, might be impacting your decisions?

Is your subconscious mind at risk from absorbing the views of biased politicians, business leaders, colleagues, influencers, conspiracy theorists, merchants peddling their wonder products or even con-artists bombarding your inbox and bugging you with crank calls? Be positively sceptical rather than merely accepting things at face value.

Today, we are discovering all sorts of information about what is true and upturning our assumptions on areas such as healthcare and wealth distribution. We must wisely seek truth which may not always be what it seems.

I have learned never to underestimate people. Gene Early and I became friends when we met during an unusual and amazing experience as guests of a Maasai tribe in Kenya. Any assumptions that the Maasai are a primitive race were soon squashed. The Maasai are wise, considered, community-driven and deeply caring of their natural environment. Their tribal leader, Salaton, told us upon arrival: "In our language Maa there is no word for stranger, so we welcome you as family." By the time we left, we felt like family, part of the community, and privileged to have learned from them. While self-interest often divides, elevated leadership like we experienced with the Maasai seeks truth and aims to unite not divide.

Regularly question your own truth and develop a positive scepticism. Develop at least one trustworthy relationship with someone who will reveal your assumptions, raise challenging questions about your world view, and who you trust to do it in a kind loving way. Invite them into a regular dialogue.

4. Wisdom

Can you remember being full of curiosity as a child? For me, this brings backs memories of hunting for small fish in a rock pool or the excitement with which my youngest son explores a museum. If you need to, reinvigorate your curiosity. Learn from others' experiences. Also, discover tools and techniques that help you make better decisions now and for the future. And most of all, align the knowledge you gain with your core values to increase your wisdom.

A fascinating interview guest, Dr Mansour Malik, kindly invited me at short notice to visit the birthplace of Rumi in Konya,

Turkey in December 2019. My conscious decision to allow my natural curiosity to flow led to me accepting the opportunity and rearranging my diary. Soon I found myself absorbed in a world of mosques, wailing prayers and mystic culture. I even interviewed the head of the Whirling Dervishes, a deeply inspiring relative of Rumi, and a hotel chain manager whose exceptional customer service turned out to be based around Rumi's wisdom. Rumi wrote "In generosity and helping others, be like a river" and when my flight home was delayed for two days by fog, I could not have been cared for in a more generous way.

The work of Rumi and experiences with these unique individuals also reconfirmed to me that to change the world we must change ourselves. As Rumi wrote: "When I was clever, I wanted to change the world, now I am wise, I am changing myself."

Make it your mission to develop your wisdom through research and experiences. For example, my online radio series and podcast, *The Business Elevation Show*, was a conscious decision to enable myself and my listeners to learn and then act on the wisdom of exceptional leaders. Seek out books, articles and podcasts and ensure that when you're available you dedicate a portion of that time to learning.

Identify someone you consider wise. Ask yourself: 'What is one expression of their wisdom that I could take, embody and act on?' Identify three actions that would be expressions of this wisdom. Then reflect on what you learned from each experience. Do this regularly and you will increase your own wisdom quotient.

5. Action

When it comes to taking action, consider the old Zen saying, 'walk not wobble'! Or as I recovered from self-inflicted injuries to my heels from participating in the Great Kindrochit Quadrathalon (a fabulous Scottish endurance event and one of the best days of my life), I now call it 'walk not hobble'.

My co-author and I, Dr Steven Levinson shared the principles of action in our book, *The Power to Get Things Done (Whether You Feel Like It or Not)*.

Learn to get into action each day and create situations that mean that you act whether you feel like it or not. Keep up the momentum by seeking people and situations that keep you so accountable that you can walk forward with only very occasional wobbles or hobbles!

Identify three key actions that will take you towards your vision each day and reflect on the three things you achieved the day before. Create a strategy for your projects that mean you have to act whether you feel like it or not!

Each week take 30 minutes to review the past week, identifying what went well and the experiences you will take on to next week. Then plan the following week. Do this and you will be surprised at how much progress you have made and how energising it is in helping you to keep moving your initiatives forward.

Summary

Understand that your contribution starts with you, build on your humility, seek a deeper understanding of truth, acquire wisdom, and act consistently. Elevate your own leadership so that the choices you act upon and the people you engage build a ripple that contributes to a better world.

CHRIS COOPER

Chris Cooper is a business elevation strategist, mentor and facilitator who transforms leaders, teams and builds highly engaged workforces. He is renowned for his deep presence, facilitation of transformational conversations and extensive global network.

Chris has hosted the weekly *Business Elevation Show* on Voice America since 2011 and is frequently interviewed by media. A fellow of the Professional Speaking Association (UK) he speaks on topics such as 'Elevating Leadership', 'Engagement', and his co-authored book *The Power to Get Things Done : Whether You Feel Like It or Not* (published by Penguin Random House (New York)). Chris previously held a variety of senior leadership roles at Punch, United Biscuits and Mars Inc. and co-founded a £3m turnover consultancy.

His latest venture *The Elevation Collective* is an exclusive network for international change-makers.

Website: www.chriscooper.co.uk

LinkedIn: https://www.linkedin.com/in/chrisdcooper

Business Elevation show:
https://www.voiceamerica.com/show/1959

THE CODE OF REACHING EXCELLENCE

AKHTAR KHAN

Time is precious. You wouldn't be reading this book unless you
wanted to reach excellence. That's why you're here. Luckily for you,
a roadmap with the tools you need to do this is inside this chapter.
Taking your knowledge, strategies, and goals and executing them
is crucial to success in your business and personal life. the 'Code
of Reaching Excellence' (CORE) is a proven system that helps you
overcome hidden obstacles and gives you the tools to execute them.

I will reveal how I've helped thousands of entrepreneurs achieve
incredible success after years of being stuck, hitting plateaus or just
settling for mediocre results. You may be moments away from one
of the most significant breakthroughs of your life. By mastering
CORE, you will discover the winning methodology behind how
successful people do the work, level up and reach excellence!

This chapter will get you to rethink aspects of your life and business that are running on autopilot. Now all I'm offering is the truth. You've probably seen the movie *The Matrix*. If you haven't, see it. Now. One of my favourite parts of the film is where Morpheus offers Neo a choice. Morpheus holds out two pills: one red, one blue. With the blue pill, Neo continues living in sweet, comfortable ignorance, but deep down he will always feel – but never know why – that something is wrong and something more is out there.

With the red pill, Neo learns that what he's been told to believe is a lie. The truth is that humans are connected to a giant computer that creates a virtual reality for the mind while using their sleeping bodies as fuel for robots ruling the world. Neo chooses the red pill. He disconnects from the machine, wakes up and begins to see the truth.

Similarly, everyone operates their life according to a code or script that creates their reality. Our habits, thought patterns, and conditioning from our past – family, friends, media, society – create a framework in our mindset which creates our reality. I call these codes a 'frame of reality'.

What Got You Here Won't Get You There

To level up our businesses and personal lives, we must upgrade our frames of reality. That means changing our self-identity, beliefs, emotional responses, habits, and actions to do the work we need. This is easier said than done. Why? Because many of us are carrying around deeply-held limiting beliefs about ourselves and buried emotional wounds that cause resistance as entrepreneurs. By resistance, I mean stress, fear, procrastination, overwhelm, doubt, a crisis in confidence, imposter syndrome and shiny penny syndrome. All of which surface when we are out of our comfort zone.

We may not have had control of the circumstances in our past that caused these beliefs and wounds. However, we can upgrade our frames of reality. If we don't upgrade them, we will unconsciously self-sabotage and hold ourselves back without even knowing.

Just like *The Matrix*. Society has been conditioning us. From a young age, we are taught to learn, remember, and recite information to pass exams, get jobs and work as a cog in the societal system. We haven't been taught how to execute and put things into practice. We haven't been taught how to be entrepreneurs. This leads us to have a false sense of achievement and believe the old cliché that knowledge is power. Knowledge alone won't get you far. Knowledge is of no value unless you can put it into practice. So, if knowledge is power, then execution is a SUPERPOWER! Using both is critical to reaching excellence.

The Four Phases of Entrepreneurship

The 'Four Phases of Entrepreneurship' is a model I created based on my own experiences and mentoring thousands of people over the last 20 years. To successfully level up in any area of your business or life, you will need to upgrade your frame of reality as you go through four phases. Whenever we learn and implement new skills or strategies, we experience different psychological and emotional responses to varying stages of the entrepreneurial journey that we go through.

Let's take a closer look at each of the four stages of entrepreneurship. When you know what's ahead of you, you can avoid getting hijacked by your old frames of reality which will cause resistance and self-sabotage.

Stage 1 – Euphoria phase – You start a new business or strategy, perhaps join a mastermind. It's exciting, unique, and inspiring, and you are full of enthusiasm with high hopes. Moreover, many people get addicted to this phase because it feels good, and it's a buzz. This phase often creates a false sense of achievement. Just because you've started a new venture or are in a mastermind or course doesn't guarantee your success.

In this stage, you have unconscious incompetence. You don't know what you don't know. In other words, you don't know how to do something and do not recognise the path to learning it. We don't see the degree of our incompetence.

Stage 2 – Epiphany phase – You get down to work. This stage is where you are out of your comfort zone and encounter resistance. You wake up and realise this will take a lot more effort and hard work than you thought. You also start to become aware that there are gaps in your knowledge and skills. There are things that you don't fully know and understand. Your ego gets wounded, making you feel inadequate or foolish. You may feel like an imposter like someone's going to expose you. At this point, people feel uncomfortable at best, pain at worst. People will often seek out a new or different strategy that they think will be easier, hence shiny penny syndrome.

Why does this happen? You now have conscious incompetence. You know that you don't know. We are now aware that we are at the beginning of a long learning curve, and you recognise the gaps in your skill and knowledge. Some people will self-sabotage, give up entirely, go back to what they were doing beforehand, and rationalise their decision, even if it's going back to something they hated. Why? Because they want to distract themselves from the pain and go back to experiencing the pleasurable feelings in the euphoria phase.

Stage 3 – Evolution phase – This is where people break through the resistance, start getting the results they want, causing their confidence and self-belief to grow. At this phase, they have conscious competence. You know how to do something, but doing it requires focus and concentration. To reach this stage, you must first welcome and work through the uncomfortable feelings that accompany stage 1. If you commit yourself to consistently doing the work, getting outside support, being compassionate towards yourself, you will break through, level up and get results.

By observing your progress, your confidence will grow, and you will feel somewhat competent in your ability. In other words, you evolve, and new frames of reality develop. In this phase, the strategy becomes more comfortable and easier to implement for continued and improved results. However, sometimes people will get too comfortable, hit a plateau and stop growing.

Stage 4 – Excellence phase – Finally, you have something to show for all your hard work. At this stage, you have unconscious competence. The real magic occurs at this final stage of the CORE transformation. From self-doubt, procrastination, discomfort, and all of the resistance experienced in stages 1 and 2, through the committed level efforts of doing the work in stage 3, emerges a new belief system and a new skill set. You develop a new identity and frame of reality. In this phase, a conscious focus is no longer needed to perform a skill or strategy smoothly. This automatic response allows us to enter an absorbed, thoughtless state, often called 'in the zone' or 'in the flow-state'. Just like driving a car when you've been driving for years, you drive without really thinking about it. You know how to do something so well that it has become 'second nature' and you can do it quickly and easily.

But you're not finished yet. Here, you need to review what you've done and search out ways you can improve. This helps you keep momentum and offers the opportunity to refocus on new or enhanced goals and strategies. This phase is really about adopting the mindset and attitude of excellence. Without continually developing, you're likely to hit a plateau or glass ceiling. You are back to feeling comfortable again as your comfort zone has grown. But left unchecked, comfort will become the enemy of progress.

The reality is that most people will not progress from stage 2 to stage 3 of the four stages of entrepreneurship. When most people become conscious of the gaps in their knowledge, they experience resistance, causing them to be brought out of their comfort zone. You see, most people struggle because of their limiting beliefs and wounds in their current frame of reality. This will either trigger a fight or flight response causing them to retreat to their comfort zone or to abandon learning the goal or strategy. They get shiny penny syndrome, where they will seek out a new strategy that they think is easier and will feel better.

It's crucial that you understand this model and have the right mentor who will help you through the challenging stages of the four stages of entrepreneurship and help you break through the barriers that are holding you back. It doesn't matter how much strategy or how much knowledge you have. You haven't fully learned a skill until you can execute it – to achieve it, you need to do the work. For this reason, I came up with CORE, a 'red pill' for entrepreneurs to break through the hidden barriers and get results fast.

Ultimately, these CORE principles will save you a lot of wasted time, pain, stress and overwhelm and help you develop bold confidence that will get you faster results. The principles in this chapter will give you the ultimate EDGE to break through the hidden barriers in entrepreneurship and reach excellence in all areas of your life, but the choice is yours.

Remember Morpheus? "All I'm offering is the truth. Nothing more."

AKHTAR KHAN

Akhtar Khan is a renowned and respected high-performance, property and business success coach. As a successful business investor, property entrepreneur and authority on mindset, Akhtar's ongoing mission is to support others in building wealth through property and business so that they can live life on their terms.

Growing up in a dysfunctional single-parent family with minimal financial resources, Akhtar discovered that a lack of resources was less important than an attitude of resourcefulness, coupled with a healthy mindset of possibility and good old hard work.

With no personal funds, experience or track record, Akhtar built a multi-million-pound portfolio that generated him a six figure income that allowed him to retire at the ripe age of 37.

Akhtar has completed over 200 property deals and is responsible for helping countless others (including many prominent, well-known experts in the industry) succeed in property and business.

Website: www.reachingexcellence.com

THE TRUTH IS ASKING FOR HELP IS A SIGN OF STRENGTH NOT WEAKNESS

ADAM STRONG

When you were growing up, did society condition you to think that you had to go to school, get good grades, get a well-paid job and live happily ever after? Well, I thought that was the right thing to be happy and successful. For some, that works, but for me I always felt like I was a black sheep, someone that didn't quite fit into society. I see friends and family in jobs or run businesses they eventually fall out of passion for, they get comfortable because of the money which takes them down a path of misery and incongruence.

Choosing entrepreneurship was an easy choice for me; however, it's not an easy route to take.

This chapter is dedicated to the established business owners and entrepreneurs out there that grind, persevere and believe in themselves every day.

Choose Purpose Over Profit

I know how difficult it can be to run a business, you want to keep your clients happy and give them the best service you can offer so they tell others. The big problem with this is that you get sucked into a loop-hole and forget about why you created your company and what it stands for.

The truth is you end up creating a job and not enjoying the freedom and reaping the rewards that you could have being a business owner or entrepreneur.

You must create a personal purpose and a company purpose in which both must be aligned.

It is the critical connection between a purpose-driven culture and business success. Your purpose should be designed to energise and engage your team, promote creativity and innovation, and help create a competitive advantage.

If you combine this by solving your clients'/customers' pain points, they start to spread the word like wildfire. It doesn't mean that profits are not important, it just means if you nail what your purpose is then profits will follow suit.

At the age of 24, I started a sports performance coaching business, working with individuals who wanted to train for sports events and those suffering with pain and injuries. It was my dream of helping individuals with their health and energy. After eight years or so I woke up one day feeling lost and confused. Life became frustrating, it felt like struggling through quicksand. The real breakthrough happened when I decided to step back and examine what my purpose was. After downscaling it gave me the time to really find what my purpose was in life.

Here are some simple questions that you need to answer which will help you establish your purpose:

1. What's important to you?

2. What are your strengths and weaknesses?

3. What are you passionate about?

4. What are the three main problems you are trying to solve?

5. Why is it important to your audience?

6. Does your audience care?

7. Are your ideal clients willing to pay you to help you solve the problem?

We were recently asked to briefly consult and mastermind with some senior board members of a financial firm. They had enjoyed some growth over a number of years but were experiencing a plateau in that growth. The board were bickering, causing conflict, and not surprisingly finding that the values of those leaders were not aligned to each other and not aligned to the values of the company. This caused disruption and a rift; we provided them with a strategy to create synchronicity and alignment allowing them to grow by showing them how to prioritise purpose over profit.

What is your personal and company purpose? Take out a sheet of paper and answer the questions above.

Cultivate a Culture of Great People

I believe that to get the best out of people you have to create a culture which makes your team feel part of something, that they are making a difference in the world; they need to feel a sense of belonging. Most people are not motivated by money, they are motivated by their purpose. I know that to build a company you must bring in individuals who share common values with your company values, otherwise it's simply not going to work. You must also learn how to help others achieve their goals in order to help you achieve yours, and provide them with necessary tools and resources. Gary Ridge, who is the CEO of the company WD40 quoted in a recent interview we did (you may know their products as the yellow and blue can), said: "A strong culture = Belief + Commitment. Don't become a soul-sucking CEO that creates fear, insecurity and ego. It's not about you, it's about the people."

You Must Learn How to Build a Tribe!

A tribe is the basic building block of any large human effort; it is greater than that of any team, superstar employees and entire companies. Seth Godin said: "A tribe is a group of people connected to one another, connected to a leader and connected to the idea."

Tribes are a community of die-hard fans, brand evangelists and activists that have one thing holding them together: you.

There are five key areas you need to focus on when building a tribe:

1. Your vision, which encapsulates what you want your business to be at some point in the future. You can use this simple formula when creating a vision.

   Vision = Passion + Believability + Imagination - Limiting Beliefs

2. You must create cohesion and collaborative relationships that work towards a common goal as a whole

3. Your tribe must have an identity

4. You must identify ideal members of your tribe. There are three:

   - Field recruits: These are the core of your tribe, the everyday person. These people help do the grassroots work of getting your message out by talking to other communities they are part of and friends and family.

   - Ambassadors: Ambassadors are your brand evangelists. They love what you do, buy what you sell, share what you tell and want to help support you and the tribe. They champion the brand and the tribe and engage as much as they can.

   - Torch Bearers: Influencers, authoritative figures, and leaders can quickly spread your brand and tribe through their own platforms. They usually have a working platform that enables them to engage with their own supporters. These are vital members of your tribe, where you can borrow their platform to share your mission

5. You must learn to cultivate and nurture that tribe by engaging and getting them involved.

A great example is the online shoe retailer Zappos. Founded in 1999, their CEO Tony Hsieh wanted to create a company that was different from other shoe retailers. Their focus was on delivering 'wow'. If you were a customer and ordered shoes through Zappos they gave you free delivery and returns, customer service reps that were not under pressure to complete so many calls in an hour and gave away free flip-flops with every order. Tony pioneered the concept of paying off new and unhappy employees $2000 to quit to maintain a level of happiness and productivity. They created a tribe based around their 10 core values and proved that purpose can lead to higher profits.

There is No Place for Micromanagement

I know easier said than done, but for years I believed it was quicker, easier and more efficient to do everything myself. It's your business, you built it, you put the sweat, blood and tears into it, no one knows how hard you have worked. The truth is micromanaging is the opposite to leadership. If you want to grow, you have to learn to let go and empower others, let your team take some of the responsibilities and burden of running a business. It makes no sense to become the jack of all trades and master of none. Micromanaging is toxic and breeds distrust in your company. The reality is that change is hard! It requires a shift in your mindset. Here are a few ways to transition to become a better leader:

1. Have a clear image in your head of what you want done

2. Communicate your expectations of them

3. Empower them and let them come up with the ideas

4. Use praise and appreciation (it goes a long way)

5. Provide and ask for constructive feedback

6. Be open to learning and growing

7. Live by your core values every day

Be Open to Learning and Growing

I believe coaching and mentoring is like oxygen; you can't survive very long without it. Many of you reading this think that you know everything when it comes to running a business. The reality is you don't, it's simply not possible. There are areas in the business you probably enjoy more than others, whether that be connecting with people, marketing, branding or knowing your numbers. You must focus on your strengths and delegate your weaknesses.

There is a difference between coaches and mentors. Coaches hold you to account and get more involved in your business whereas a mentor is more of an advisor that offers counsel and advice.

The truth is you can move faster and quicker by learning from others that have been there and done the journey that you aim to embark on. I remember my first coach; his name was Alex McGee. I was introduced to him on my first visit to the athletics track. Alex was in his late 50s, had a huge amount of success back in the day. What I loved about him was the fact he could take an average kid like me and turn them into champions. He was a great coach because he chose me, he saw potential that I didn't see. There are many so-called coaches out there; here is a checklist to use when considering taking one on:

1. Has the individual owned or managed a business before?

2. Do they have a great track record?

3. Do they have clients' testimonials and reviews? Are they willing to introduce you to some of their clients?

4. Do they put your interests first?

5. Are they knowledgeable about how to solve your problem?

6. Do they match your core values?

7. Are they congruent with what they say and do? (Especially on social media)

8. Do they inspire you to be better?

9. Do you have a good feeling about them (what does your gut instinct say?)

The difference between good and great coaches is that great coaches choose who they wish to work with.

Summary

The reality is that asking for help is a sign of strength, not weakness. Why try to work things out on your own when you can have access to an abundance of expertise around you. It doesn't have to be a coach; it could be a family member or friend. I know that by surrounding yourself with the five most common people you hang out with is who you become. Choose wisely.

ADAM STRONG

Adam Strong is a serial entrepreneur, international speaker and author. He runs three different businesses and enjoys working with established business owners and entrepreneurs in professional services. Adam is a former elite athlete and trained with Olympic champion Sir Mo Farah for three years. He takes the same skill set that he learned as an elite athlete to teach his clients on how to increase profitability by building purpose-led, results- orientated and impactful businesses. He is the author of two books *Move it or Lose it* and *Fit Body Fit Business* and the curating author of *Play the Game*.

Adam's chart-trending podcast show *The Game Changer's Experience* shares tips and insights with business disruptors, thought leaders and athletes.

Adam became the 'Best Man' for supporting women in business in 2016, has been featured on the front cover of *Influential People Magazine*, *Steer Magazine* and *Global Man* magazine.

Contact Adam: https://linktr.ee/adamstrongofficial

Lightning Source UK Ltd.
Milton Keynes UK
UKHW040819090222
398402UK00002B/225

9 781784 529536